P. D. James

Twayne's English Authors Series

Kinley E. Roby, Editor

Northeastern University

TEAS 430

P. D. JAMES
Photograph by Jerry Bauer

P. D. James

By Richard B. Gidez

Pennsylvania State University

Twayne Publishers • Boston

P. D. James

Richard B. Gidez

Copyright © 1986 by G.K. Hall & Co.
All Rights Reserved
Published by Twayne Publishers
A Division of G.K. Hall & Co.
70 Lincoln Street
Boston, Massachusetts 02111

Copyediting supervised by Lewis DeSimone
Book production by Elizabeth Todesco
Book design by Barbara Anderson

Typeset in 11 pt. Garamond
by P&M Typesetting, Inc., Waterbury, Connecticut

Printed on permanent/durable acid-free paper
and bound in the United States of America

Library of Congress Cataloging in Publication Data

Gidez, Richard B.
  P.D. James

  (Twayne's English authors series; TEAS 430)
  Bibliography: p. 148
  Includes index.
  1. James, P. D.—Criticism and interpretation.
2. Detective and mystery stories, English—History and
criticism. I. Title. II. Series.
PR6060.A467Z68 1986   823'.914   86-3073
ISBN 0-8057-6924-2

16

Contents

About the Author
Preface
Acknowledgments
Chronology

P. D. JAMES

About the Author

Richard B. Gidez received his degrees from Harvard University, Columbia University, and Ohio State University. He has taught at Ohio State and the Pennsylvania State University where he is an associate professor in English and American studies. He has been a bibliographer for the Modern Language Association of America and has published in *The Shaw Review, Seventeenth-Century News*, and the *Journal of General Education*. He has also contributed biographical and critical essays on Enid Bagnold, Ronald Harwood, and Emlyn Williams for *Modern British Dramatists 1900–1945* and *Modern British Dramatists Since World War II*.

Preface

P. D. James (Phyllis Dorothy James White) did not publish her first novel, a mystery, until 1962, when she was forty-two years old. Since 1949, she had worked for the Hospital Service in England, leaving there in 1968 to work for the Home Office, first in the police department and then in the criminal department, until her retirement in 1979. During these years, she continued to write and publish her fiction.

James's output of fiction is small—nine novels in twenty-two years, all but one mysteries in the mode of the classical English detective novel, and a handful of short stories. By comparison, Dick Francis and Ruth Rendell, two other English writers of mysteries whose reputations rival that of James, have published far more. Francis, who is James's age and whose first novel also appeared in 1962, has twenty-four novels to his name; Rendell, who is James's junior by ten years and whose first novel appeared in 1964, has twenty-four novels and three collections of short stories to her credit.

Despite her few titles, James has achieved the position of one of the foremost writers of crime fiction. Robert Barnard, writing in the *Armchair Detective*, cites James and Rendell as "the two foremost practitioners of the traditional detective story." Clifton Fadiman considers James, Francis, and John le Carré "three English masters of the thriller who have broken through. They write fiction good enough on other counts to attract a general novel reading public."[1] To readers, writers, and reviewers, she is the successor to the mantle of Agatha Christie who died in 1976.

The comparison to Christie is both flattering and misleading. It is flattering in the sense that Agatha Christie and the detective novel are almost synonymous. More than anyone else, Christie shaped the murder mystery into the form that has become standard since her first book, *The Mysterious Affair at Styles*, in 1920. It was Christie who popularized so many of the conventions readers have come to expect as essential to the "whodunit": the baffling crime, the intriguing setting, the closed circle of suspects, the trivial detail that furnishes the all important clue, the red herring, the detective of superior intelligence, the ingenious solution. These elements are characteristic of the mysteries of P. D. James as well.

The difference between the two writers—and it is a major difference—is their goals. Christie never thought of her mysteries as anything more than superior entertainments. To this end, she placed her emphasis on the puzzle and would deceive her readers right up to the last page with complicated twists and dazzling surprises. Her wooden characters exist to serve the plot. Social questions and issues of the day seldom, if ever, intrude into her fictional world.

James, however, sees her work as being no different from that of any other novelist, except that she is working within the genre of the formal detective story. She puts her emphasis not on the puzzle but on her characters, real men and women, and the problems they face: making a living, maintaining a relationship, and dealing with the crises of everyday life, as well as being suspects and witnesses in a murder investigation. The world James's characters inhabit is far more recognizable than that of Christie's characters.

Moreover, James's detectives, Adam Dalgliesh and Cordelia Gray, though no less brilliant at solving crimes than Christie's Hercule Poirot and Jane Marple, are, at the same time, more believable, more vulnerable, and more capable of development from book to book. They are of as much interest themselves as the crimes they investigate and solve.

It is, perhaps, more appropriate to look at James in the company of Dorothy L. Sayers and Margery Allingham, Christie's best known contemporaries. Like Sayers, James has shifted the emphasis from the puzzle to the creation of credible characters, whom she depicts with a good deal of psychological insight. Like Allingham, James has brought to her fiction a brilliant sense of place and an acute awareness of what can happen to people who have reached the breaking point. Like both Sayers and Allingham at their best, James has stretched and extended the range of the mystery story so that her fiction reads more like a traditional novel than like a detective thriller.

James has acknowledged the influence of both Sayers and Allingham. But James deserves to be examined on her own merits and not as the successor to Christie or Sayers or Allingham. Robert Barnard, writing of Ruth Rendell—like James, she has often been nominated for the Christie mantle—wisely points out that these "backward comparisons" are not helpful, for mystery writers of an earlier generation "created an artificial world whose relation to the real one was at best tangential." By comparison, Rendell and James "bring to popular crime fiction minds that are nourished and motivated by the social realities of Britain today."[2]

The bulk of this study is a descriptive and critical analysis of the fiction of P. D. James from her first novel, *Cover Her Face* in 1962 to her most recent work, *The Skull Beneath the Skin* in 1982. There is also a consideration of her short stories, which have received little, if any, critical attention. Only her one book of nonfiction, *The Maul and the Pear Tree* (1971), written in collaboration with Thomas A. Critchley, is not discussed. This examination of the "Radcliffe Highway Murders" has been published in the United States too recently— Spring 1986—to be included for analysis in this study.

The study begins with a biographical sketch of P. D. James and with a look at the classical English detective story, both to see where James's roots lie and how she has revitalized a genre many readers of mystery fiction had thought dead and how she has made it come as alive as any contemporary novel.

One caveat to the reader. It is impossible to describe and discuss James's fiction at any length and in any detail without giving away turns of plot and identities of murderers. Because endings are so important in detective fiction, the endings of James's novels are, regretfully, revealed. But as anyone who has read a novel by P. D. James can testify, there is much more to her fiction than the solution to a puzzling crime. It is with that "much more" that this study is concerned.

Richard B. Gidez

Pennsylvania State University

Acknowledgments

The following excerpts are reprinted with the permission of Charles Scribner's Sons:

P. D. James, excerpted from *The Black Tower.* © 1975 P. D. James.

P. D. James, excerpted from *Cover Her Face.* © 1962 P. D. James.

P. D. James, excerpted from *Crime Times Three.* © 1979 P. D. James.

P. D. James, excerpted from *Death of an Expert Witness.* © 1977 P. D. James.

P. D. James, excerpted from *Innocent Blood.* © 1980 P. D. James.

P. D. James, excerpted from *A Mind to Murder.* © 1963 P. D. James.

P. D. James, excerpted from *Murder in Triplicate.* Introduction © 1980 P. D. James.

P. D. James, excerpted from *Shroud for a Nightingale.* © 1971 P. D. James.

P. D. James, excerpted from *The Skull beneath the Skin.* © 1982 P. D. James.

P. D. James, excerpted from *Unnatural Causes.* © 1967 P. D. James.

P. D. James, excerpted from *An Unsuitable Job for a Woman.* © 1972 P. D. James.

Thanks to Charles Scribner's Sons for permission to reprint the frontispiece of P. D. James by Jerry Bauer.

I am indebted to Martha Kolln for her many wise and always helpful comments on the manuscript.

Chronology

1977 *Death of an Expert Witness* published in England and the United States; chosen as an alternate selection of the Book-of-the-Month Club.

1980 *Innocent Blood* published in England and the United States; chosen as a main selection of the Book-of-the-Month Club.

1982 *The Skull beneath the Skin* published in England and the United States; chosen as part of a dual selection of the Book-of-the-Month Club.

1983 Made an Officer of the Order of the British Empire.

1984 Teaches a course on the art of the detective story at Boston University's Metropolitan College.

Chapter One

P. D. James and the English Classic Mystery

Phyllis Dorothy James was born in Oxford, England, on 3 August 1920, to Sidney James, a middle-grade civil servant who worked for Inland Revenue, and Amelia Hone James. Two other children, a boy and a girl, were to follow at eighteen month intervals. Born in one university city, she grew up and was educated in another, Cambridge, where the family moved in 1931 after a time in Ludlow on the Welsh border. She attended Cambridge Girls' High School from 1931–37. In 1972 she wrote about Cambridge in *An Unsuitable Job for a Woman*. In an author's note making the customary acknowledgment that the characters are imaginary, she adds, "the city, happily for us all, is not." She considers the city of Cambridge "one of the loveliest in Europe."[1]

Although James wanted to attend college, higher education was not then government subsidized and, more to the point, her father was not disposed to education for girls. Still, she did read widely in the English novel, especially Jane Austen, George Eliot, and Anthony Trollope. Upon graduating from high school at age sixteen, she worked for a few years in a tax office where, she remembers, she was absolutely miserable. She soon found a position more to her liking, as assistant stage manager at Cambridge's Festival Theatre selling tickets and fetching and carrying for staff and actors.

A few days after her twenty-first birthday, she married Ernest Connor Bantry White, a young medical student at Cambridge, who served as a doctor during World War II with the Royal Army Medical Corps. Their first daughter, Clare, was born in 1942; the second, Jane, in 1944. Jane was named after her mother's favorite author, Jane Austen—also the favorite author, not surprisingly, of James's detective Adam Dalgliesh. During the final days before giving birth, James was reading Austen in a London bomb shelter. Outside, nightmare and chaos raged—the devastation of London by the Nazi V-1 rocket bombings; inside, she was immersed in Austen's "blessed atmosphere of sanity and peace,"[2] perhaps *Emma*, her favorite Austen novel. James has called *Emma* "a magnificent detective story, one of the best ever written, except it hasn't got a murderer at the centre of it."[3]

Upon discharge from military service, Dr. White was able to practice only sporadically; mental illness, probably schizophrenia, cut short his career. Much of his time until his death in 1964 was spent in mental hospitals. Because the authorities would never acknowledge that his illness was the result of his war service, he received no pension after the war. James, with two daughters to raise, became a clerk in the National Health Service. She also began attending evening classes, earning two diplomas, one in hospital administration, the other in medical research. In 1949 she took a job as an administrative assistant, doing mental health work at the North West Regional Hospital Board in London. Later she became a fellow of the Institute of Hospital Administration. In both positions she gained experience that provided her with detailed knowledge of illness, invalidism, and the running of institutions that she uses with great skill and authority in her mysteries.

A New Career

Although as a child James had decided to be a novelist, the circumstances of her life intervened: early marriage and motherhood and her husband's ill health all stood in the way. But as her fortieth birthday approached, she told herself very determinedly that if she did not begin to write soon, she never would. Not wanting to be "one of those failed writers who never got down to it," she got down to it.[4]

Cover Her Face, James's first novel, took almost every minute of her free time for three years before she completed it in 1960. She wrote between six and eight A.M. before going to work, a regimen she kept to even after she retired as a fulltime administrator. Her creativity functioned best in the hours before breakfast, stimulated and sustained by that all-important first cup of tea. Evenings she used for planning, research, and revision. The book was published in England in 1962 by Faber and Faber and in the United States in 1966 by Charles Scribner's Sons, her American publisher since then. She chose to use her maiden name on this and subsequent books because

"James" was "the essential me and my family name from the beginning."[5] She chose the initials P. D. because she thought an author's sex should not be of concern to people. She wanted to be judged simply as a writer.

Upon her husband's death in 1964, James decided to broaden her horizons by changing positions. When the Home Office wanted to extend its base of recruitment of senior people, she took its highly competitive exams, electing as her special interest the criminal department. From 1968 through 1979, when she retired, she was a civil servant with the Home Office. The oldest of the British departments of state, the Home Secretary's Office combines the functions of the United States Department of Interior and the Justice Department. James worked at formulating criminal law policy, becoming a specialist in juvenile delinquency. Her tenure with the Home Office gave her a solid grounding in police procedures and law; and it provided the authenticity that is apparent in her depiction of the routines of a forensic science laboratory in *Death of an Expert Witness* (1977).

During these years in the Home Office she kept writing. Never once did she receive a rejection slip, a situation that shook her children's confidence in her books; they felt that good novels should be turned down.[6]

In 1971 James collaborated with a fellow official at the Home Office, Thomas A. Critchley, on her only book of nonfiction. *The Maul and the Pear Tree* deals with the Radcliffe Highway Murders in London's East End in 1811, the subject of Thomas De Quincey's famous essay, "On Murder Considered as One of the Fine Arts" (1827). The book has been published only recently (1986) in the United States.

James also wrote several stories, one of which, "Moment of Power," won first prize in the *Ellery Queen Mystery Magazine* competition in 1968. Two of her mystery novels have received the British Crime Writers Association Silver Dagger award: *Shroud for a Nightingale* in 1971 and *The Black Tower* in 1975. The former also won an Edgar from the Mystery Writers of America; in 1973 *An Unsuitable Job for a Woman* received a scroll from the same organization.

James's last two books, *Innocent Blood* (1980), her only nonmystery novel, and *The Skull beneath the Skin* (1982), were both chosen as main selections of the Book-of-the-Month Club, an honor shared by only a few other writers of mysteries, Dick Francis and Ruth Rendell. Both books were best sellers: The paperback rights for *Innocent Blood* sold for $313,000, with a movie deal rumored at an estimated $350,000; the paperback edition of *The Skull beneath the Skin* was launched with a $50,000 major promotional campaign. With an estimated four million copies of her books in print, James's critical and financial success clearly justify the title *Newsweek* gave her in 1978: "a new Queen of crime."[7]

P. D. James has been honored in her homeland as well. In the summer of 1983 she appeared on the Queen's birthday honors list, and she is now an Officer of the Order of the British Empire.

Her Method of Writing

More often than not, the idea for a story comes to James from a place: "a desolate stretch of coast, an old and sinister house, an atmospheric part of London, a closed community such as a Nurses Home, a village, a forensic science laboratory." The idea will germinate for weeks, even months, and as it does, it will become fleshed out with characters and plot ("literally the plot thickens," she says). "It is almost as if the whole book and the people already exist in some limbo outside myself and it is my business, by a long process of thought and effort, to get in touch with them and put them down on paper."[8]

In putting her ideas down on paper, she does not begin with the first chapter and work straight through to the concluding one. Rather, she sees the book as if it were a film, a series of scenes that, depending on her mood at the time, can be written in any order. Some mornings she might feel like a dose of violence; on other mornings, perhaps because of the weather, she might feel like a bit of description. "Some mornings I am attracted to dialogue, perhaps to scenes where my detective is interviewing suspects and there is the cut and thrust of verbal confrontation."[9]

Such a method, obviously, assumes that the author meticulously plan the book down to the last clue and suspect. And that is exactly what she does. James carefully works out the kind of weather, the setting, the clues, and the red herrings. Although characters and plot turns may change during the writing, there is a basic structure that controls the book. James even keeps an hour-by-hour chart so that she can see where each of her suspects is at the time of the murder.

This attention to detail lifts her mysteries from the routine formula of so many traditional detective stories.

Why Mysteries

When James took up writing, there was no question in her mind that she would write detective stories. She had always enjoyed reading mysteries, so thought she might enjoy writing them. Working in such a popular genre would also give her the best opportunity to be published. Above all other considerations, however, she was drawn to writing mysteries because she placed a very high premium on construction in a novel. She was fascinated by the challenge of shaping a plot with all sorts of intriguing tensions among action, characters, and atmosphere. The disciplined form of the detective story, with its strong emphasis on a beginning, middle, and end, could provide a successful apprenticeship for someone who had hopes of becoming a serious novelist.

James certainly did not believe the detective story to be a substandard genre relying on contrivance, nor did she believe mystery writers to be second-class citizens sacrificing psychological truths to the demands of plot. Mystery writers, she told *Newsweek*, are getting away from feeling their books are "inferior to straight novels."[10] What they are writing is very real fiction to them. She herself resists the notion that even though her books are thrillers they can be dismissed as mere entertainments. She argues that a writer can say something about complex personal relationships, about how people behave under the ultimate stress of death, and do so in a popular genre like the detective story. More than one critic has agreed with her assessment: Newgate Callendar says that she is "basically a novelist who happens to put her characters into mystery stories."[11]

Contemporary writers of detective fiction blur the distinction between detective novels and serious fiction. They give readers, insists Jessica Mann, herself a popular crime novelist, "something more than pleasantly intellectual stimulation." They also cast a "dispassionate eye as much upon the passion, as upon the deed it produced." Like writers of straight fiction, detective novelists "touch the heights and depths of human passion as well."[12] Certainly writers such as P. D. James, Ruth Rendell, Celia Fremlin, and Margaret Millar take the classical detective story and make it come as alive as any contemporary novel.

The Value of Detective Fiction

One of the great values of the detective story, according to James, is that it gives "an extraordinary realistic picture of what life was like at the time it was written much more so than many serious novels."[13] In accounting for the continued popularity of Dorothy L. Sayers's mysteries, James notes how clearly they reflect their period. "Perhaps because clue-making so often involves the routine and minutiae of ordinary life, the detective novel can tell us more about contemporary society than many a more pretentious literary form."[14] What she means, of course, goes beyond the mere learning of details of the theatre from Ngaio Marsh or horse racing from Dick Francis or banking from Emma Lathen or orchids from Rex Stout. It is also learning about the mores and manners of Southern California from Ross Mac-Donald and the racial antagonisms and tensions in South Africa from James McClure, the role of environment in the molding of character from Dorothy Salisbury Davis, and insights into life among the ill and dying from P. D. James.

In mystery fiction, moreover, one can find the imposition of a moral order that is too often missing from contemporary society. Even though one may feel "impotent in the face of violence and tragedy and injustice in this world," the pattern at the end of the mystery novel does make things come out right.[15] The order that James found in the world of Jane Austen is the order the detective restores to a world whose equilibrium has been disrupted by murder. Detective fiction promises readers that the virtues of reason, sanity, and logic will triumph in the end and that evil is only a temporary lapse. Those who strongly believe that order can come out of chaos, that there is such a thing as justice, can find reassurance in detective fiction.

People who believe in society's basic and unambiguous values—that murder is wrong no matter who the victim, that even the most wretched of human beings has the right to live out his or her natural days—are affronted by murder. Since the victim cannot avenge himself, all the resources of civilized society must be brought to bear when murder is committed.[16] Society in the person of the detective upholds these values by solving the crime and bringing the murderer to justice. Detective fiction, as James has said on more than one occasion, has all the fascination of a medieval morality play.[17]

Women and Detective Fiction

The kind of detective story James writes belongs to the genre of the classical detective novel, the formal puzzle, the traditional English mystery that we associate with the golden age of detective fiction in the 1920s and 1930s. It is a genre then and now long dominated by women. Some write under their own names: Margery Allingham, Agatha Christie, Ngaio Marsh, Gladys Mitchell, Patricia Moyes, Ruth Rendall, Dorothy L. Sayers, June Thompson. Some write under female pseudonyms: Amanda Cross, Emma Lathen, Elizabeth Peters, Josephine Tey, Alice Tilton. Others write under male pseudonyms: Edward Candy, Stanton Forbes, Anthony Gilbert, Craig Rice, Joseph Shearing, Tobias Wells. Still others write under initials: R. B. Dominic, E. X. Ferrars, M. V. Heberden, P. D. James.

Why are respectable, middle-class women—a description that fits many practitioners of the genre—so good at plotting murder? It may be, according to James, because of their love of order. Constructing mysteries, she admits, is "like cutting out a dress; everything has to fit."[18] Moreover, she says women are better than men at understanding "personal feelings . . . like jealousy and hatred,"[19] the warhorses among motives in mysteries. Women are naturally skilled in dealing with "the tensions, intrigues . . . and resentments which can fester in the closed circles beloved of crime writers" and which "finally erupt into the ultimate crime."[20]

Women also have a keen eye for the domestic details of everyday life, "the nuances of human behavior and humanity,"[21] that furnish the clues that lead to the solution. "Who was where and with whom and when? Who ate the poisoned salad and who prepared it? What woman would wear that purple lipstick found near the body? Who locked the library door and when?"[22] It may also be that women have turned to literary mayhem as a means of sublimating and "of purging irrational feelings of anxiety and guilt."[23] Writing may be a therapeutic outlet for some. Clearly, these are not the motives of P. D. James; for her writing is an end in itself.

The Big Four writers of the classical English detective story are all women: Agatha Christie, Dorothy L. Sayers, Margery Allingham, and Ngaio Marsh. P. D. James is often mentioned as being in their distinguished company, and she readily acknowledges the influence of Sayers and Allingham. To understand that influence and to grasp James's accomplishments, it is necessary to examine the traditional formal mystery as practiced by the Big Four and other writers.

The Classical Detective Novel

James has succinctly isolated the elements of the formal traditional detective novel: "The central mysterious death; the closed circle of suspects, each with a credible motive; the arrival of the detective like the avenging deity of an old Morality play; the final solution which the reader himself can arrive at by logical deduction from clues presented to him with deceptive cunning but essential fairness."[24] These four elements certainly characterize the classic mystery—and certainly also the work of P. D. James.

Murder. As Jacques Barzun convincingly argues, a detective story need not involve murder. As he defines it, "The point of a detective story is the unravelling of a physical mystery in a physical way by plausible inference."[25] Although a mystery should be exciting— and what is more exciting than murder?—a corpse is not essential to the detective story. Indeed, some of the great mysteries are not murder mysteries: Edgar Allan Poe's "The Purloined Letter," Wilkie Collin's *The Moonstone*, many of the Sherlock Holmes stories, Dorothy L. Sayers's *Gaudy Night*. Still, murder is the most serious crime of all. Most formal detective stories contain at least one corpse, dispatched by a rare South African poison (Agatha Christie's *Death in the Air*, 1935) or by a chisel right through the heart (P. D. James's *A Mind to Murder*, 1967) or, in one of the most original methods of murder, a triggered piano pedal (Ngaio Marsh's *Overture to Death*, 1939).

The closed community. Often, the murder occurs in a country house or in a quaint English village. The setting for Cyril Hare's aptly titled *An English Murder* (1951) is Warbeck Hall, "the oldest inhabited house in Monkshire." Such a setting is not required, of course. Even Agatha Christie's Miss Marple leaves the quiet village of St. Mary Mead to encounter corpses at Bertram's Hotel in London and on the beaches of the Caribbean. The settings for the formal detective story are varied, indeed.

Murder can take place in special interest communities such as the theater (Ngaio Marsh's *Night at the Vulcan*, 1951) or a hospital (Christianna Brand's *Green for Danger*, 1944), or in a university's English department (Amanda Cross's *Death in a Tenured Position*, 1981), or in an advertising agency (Dorothy L. Sayers's *Murder Must Advertise*, 1933), or in a dress-making salon (Margery Allingham's *The Fashion in Shrouds*, 1938). Murder can happen in a lonely town in the Australian outbacks (Arthur Upfield's *Death of a Swagman*, 1946), or in the African bush (Elspeth Huxley's *Murder on Safari*, 1938), or at a posh dinner party in Buenos Aires (M. V. Heberden's *Engaged to Murder*, 1949). It can occur on the high seas (Bruce Hamilton's *Too Much of Water*, 1958), or on a channel airflight (Agatha Christie's *Death in the Air*, 1935), or on a New York trolley car (Ellery Queen's *The Tragedy of X*, 1932). But no matter what the setting, the writer of the traditional detective mystery constructs an enclosed universe inhabited by victim, suspects, murderer, and detective.

The advantages of the closed community are obvious enough. First, there is the fascination of watching characters in a closed society: "the power struggles, the attempt to establish and retain one's own identity, the way in which people group defensive or offensive alliances, particularly against strangers."[26] It is this closed society that the detective penetrates, creating dramatic tension as he examines it with fresh eyes and as the society reacts to him.

Second, murder in a closed community touches everyone. It forces each person to recognize the desperation or sense of extremity that can lead one to take someone else's life and perhaps to recognize that no one is free from that desperation or sense of extremity.

Third, a closed society means a closed circle of suspects, each with an appropriate motive, means, and opportunity. There should not be too many, so as to be confusing, or too few, so as to rob the reader of the pleasure of solving the puzzle. With a limited cast, the author can build excitement and tension. Each character knows that the passenger seated next to him on the train or the office mate whose desk is across the aisle or the boarder who lives down the hall might be the killer.

Finally, the closed community with its claustrophobic atmosphere is the ideal setting for brewing up a cauldron of desires and disappointments among people and for bringing to the surface emotions of envy, greed, jealousy, hatred, even love, often the most destructive force—all appropriate motives for murder.

In the mysteries of P. D. James, the closed communities are often medical settings. She finds the medical establishment ideal: "A strongly hierarchical community with its own esoteric rules and conventions; a mysterious but fascinating world of men and women performing a great variety of necessary jobs. . . . where the reader, like the patient, feels vulnerable, apprehensive and alien."[27]

The amateur sleuth. In an interview in *Publishers Weekly*, James promised never to inflict upon her readers as detective "the stereotyped English detective hero, a sprig of nobility, who is welcomed by professional police with gentle fun and subtle awe," and who eventually unmasks the murderer.[28] She had in mind, of course, the amateur gentleman sleuth so beloved of the writers of the golden age of detective fiction, a sleuth like Dorothy L. Sayers's Lord Peter Wimsey: "Independent, eccentric, brilliant, omniscient, in egregious contrast to the poorly paid, plodding, unimaginative and deferential police."[29] In her opinion, the day of the amateur sleuth, if not over, had at least reached and passed the "high noon" of his popularity.

The amateur gentleman (or lady) sleuth reigned supreme in the 1920s and 1930s. Even when their vocation was detecting, few seemed to earn a living from it, thus not endangering their amateur status. In addition to Lord Peter there were Agatha Christie's Hercule Poirot and Miss Marple, Margery Allingham's Albert Campion, rumored to be related to the royal family, and in the United States, Ellery Queen and S. S. Van Dine's Philo Vance.

To be sure, there were a few police heroes in the 1920s and 1930s: Earl Derr Biggers's Charlie Chan and Freeman Wills Crofts's Inspector French, but certainly the most popular detectives were the amateurs. Today, however, mystery writers are much more likely to settle on the professional policeman as detective as being more realistic. It is only infrequently that someone who is not a policeman runs across a corpse in a closed community.

More and more, mysteries are "rooted in the realities of human existence." More and more, they deal "perceptively with such universal absolutes as life and death, love and hate, treachery and failure." More and more, detection "is closer to the realities, the ardors, the frustrations and the disappointments of real-life criminal investigation."[30]

A policeman hero, moreover, is likely to be free of the eccentricities of manner and being that characterize the great sleuths of yesteryear, eccentricities that can and did become tiresome; Philo Vance's erudite knowledge and Régie cigarettes; Ellery Queen's immense ego and his rimless pince-nez; Hercule Poirot's little gray cells and his passion for symmetry and sweets. Christie herself tired of Poirot and his waxed moustaches, his black pointed patent leather shoes, and his little gray cells, "always the little gray cells, *mon ami.*" Dorothy L. Sayers, Margery Allingham, and Ellery Queen all changed some of the more pronounced and irritating characteristics of their detectives as the years went by. Lord Peter Wimsey, Albert Campion, and Ellery Queen metamorphosed from fatuous, foppish sleuths to more socially concerned, caring men one could turn to in times of need or trouble. Even so, Sayers gave up writing mysteries in the 1940s and Allingham grew less interested in Campion, who withdrew further back in her books (he plays only a minor part in her masterpiece, *Tiger in the Smoke*, 1952). Certainly the public—if not his creator—grew tired of the often rude and effete Philo Vance, who drove Ogden Nash to rhyme, "Philo Vance / Needs a kick in the pance."

James did not want that kind of behavior from her detective; and of course Scotland Yard would not put up with such idiosyncracies. Her detective would be neither omniscient nor omnipotent. James demanded intelligence, experience, sensitivity, and above all, the professionalism that goes with painstaking police work.

In these attributes Adam Dalgliesh, her detective, resembles many of his fictional police contemporaries: Patricia Moyes's conscientious Chief Superintendent Henry Tibbet; Ruth Rendell's very moral Chief Inspector Reginald Wexford: Michael Innes's erudite and urbane Sir John Appleby, now retired; Ngaio Marsh's gentlemanly Detective Superintendent Roderick Alleyn—like Dalgliesh, a skilled interrogator of suspects; and Josephine Tey's sophisticated and sensitive Inspector Alan Grant.

Although James obviously likes her detective—"no writer . . . continues to write about a character he or she despises or finds irritating"—she is not certain she would enjoy serving under him. "With his critical intelligence, essential self-sufficiency, his sensitivity, and low tolerance of fools, he could, I suspect, be an uncomfortable colleague."[31]

James sees the imperturbable Dalgliesh as a "very detached man . . . a very lonely man in a lonely profession, one which brings him into contact with tragedy, with *evil*."[32] He is not unlike a novelist. The novelist stands outside and observes his or her own experiences. Even at moments of tragedy the writer "is able . . . to be watching it—to be suffering, even." Like the novelist who is both in society and yet also detached and watching, Dalgliesh as he investigates feels all the pain and suffering of the human condition.[33]

Dalgliesh is a man who tracks down murderers. He is also a published poet. He is far more interesting and complex than Lord Peter Wimsey or Albert Campion. Nonetheless, he is their successor in his ability to solve baffling crimes through logical deductions from observed data.

The puzzle.   In the classic mystery the emphasis is on the puzzle. Why is all the furniture turned backwards in the room where the victim is found in Ellery Queen's *The Chinese Orange Mystery* (1934)? What is the meaning of the A. B. C. railroad guides left near the bodies of the victims in Agatha Christie's *The A. B. C. Murders* (1936)? Who is responsible for the orgy of deaths in the gloomy Greene mansion in S. S. Van Dine's *The Greene Murder Case* (1928)? Inevitably, by the final chapters, Ellery Queen, Hercule Poirot, and Philo Vance have put together all the clues, including some that even the most alert reader may have overlooked; they have threaded their way through the red herrings and traps the murderers have set; and by the powers of deduction or by means of the little gray cells or through arcane knowledge of German criminologists, they can finally point an accusing finger at the killers.

But for James it is not the puzzle that is of primary interest. Few readers, she suspects, "watch for every clue." Most "guess the murderer more through . . . knowledge of the author, his style, prejudices and foibles, than through close attention to each detail of the plot." She believes that readers pit their wits "against the writer, not his villain or his detective."[34]

Nevertheless, she is scrupulously careful in giving all the clues—and giving them fairly, she hopes. "It should be possible to reason out the solution." After all, readers of mysteries "have a right to expect that it'll be fair." At the same time, she believes strongly that the solution has to be psychologically right: It is "no good if it merely fits neatly because these are the facts. . . . Psychologically, the crime *must* arise from human nature."[35]

Dorothy L. Sayers and Margery Allingham

In seeing the detective story as something more than an ingenious puzzle, James is in the same company as the two mystery writers she most admires: Dorothy L. Sayers and Margery Allingham. Both writers, while using the familiar formula of the classic puzzle, stretched and extended the genre.

Sayers employed all the conventions of the classical detective story: false clues, timetables, alibis, and the like. Her desire, however, was to write a book that "was less like a conventional detective story and more like a novel."[36] She invented characters who are credible and engaging; she is especially good with "the shabby, the failures, the commonplace—the second-raters whose moral obtuseness just might shade off into sheer evil."[37] That she was not completely comfortable with her creations, however, is evident in the idealized love affair between Lord Peter and Harriet Vane.

Sayers did bring wit and a sense of style to the tried-and-tested ploys of detective fiction. She writes with "a refreshing humor . . . rare in detective fiction. . . . born of a keen eye and a frank relish for the vagaries, inconsistencies, and absurdities of life."[38] Her strongly drawn characters, her psychological approach, her effective sense of place, her ability to combine the detective story with the novel of social realism—all of these features of her writing advanced the detective novel beyond Agatha Christie's emphasis on plot and puzzle.

There are a number of parallels between the novels of Sayers and James, especially between *Gaudy Night* and *An Unsuitable Job for a Woman*: similarities in setting, in the names of characters, and in the situations. On the whole, however, James's powers of observation are sharper and her resolutions bleaker than those of Sayers. As Bernard Benstock tellingly points out in his essay, "The Clinical World of P. D. James": "Rarely since Sayers has a writer of thrillers diagnosed existing society with such microscopic precision" and "dissected human character with such relentlessness."[39]

Allingham, in *Tiger in the Smoke* ("probably among the best mysteries ever written," according to James),[40] moved the classic puzzle closer to the psychological thriller. The book reveals a genuine feel for the presence of evil in the world. It makes nonsense, as James writes, "of the criticism that the great absolutes of good and evil are, and must always remain, outside the mystery's range and that it is thus an essentially trivial form."[41]

James sees the mystery novel as anything but trivial. Like a stone rippling across the water's smooth surface, murder stirs up currents of emotion and fear. It raises to the surface the characters's foibles and fears. In its contaminating effect, murder alters the lives of the innocent and the guilty. The murder is always solved, but always at a cost to victim and killer, suspects and detective. This cost and its effects constitute a major theme for James from *Cover Her Face*, her first mystery, to *The Skull beneath the Skin*, her most recent. Like Sayers and Allingham, James works within the formal structure and convention of detective fiction to produce books that one can take seriously as straight fiction. Like Sayers and Allingham, she has a vivid sense of atmosphere and place, each novel with its own distinctive setting. Like Sayers and Allingham, her prose is literate, often witty, and always a pleasure to read. James's detective, Adam Dalgliesh, is in the line of his illustrious predecessors, but unlike them, he is more believable and more capable of development. P. D. James is surely the literary heir of both Sayers and Allingham. What she has said of their contribution to the classic detective story can be equally said of her own work: They "helped to raise the mystery form as sub-literary puzzle to a form with serious claims to be regarded as a novel."[42]

Chapter Two
Cover Her Face

In their *Fifty Classics of Crime Fiction, 1950–1975*, Jacques Barzun and Wendell Hertig Taylor have selected one title each from the fifty mystery writers they most liked. P. D. James is represented by her first mystery, *Cover Her Face* (London, 1962, New York, 1966).[1] Although Barzun and Taylor acknowledge that in some ways, her later books surpass her first venture into crime, they believe she "showed her quality early, in her very first book . . . just as Christie and Sayers did in theirs." Further, her first mystery offers a fresh reworking of the overly familiar "scene and plot of the English country house affair."[2]

The Maxies of Martingale

Cover Her Face is set at Martingale, a handsome Elizabethan manor home in Chadfleet, with bay windows, Tudor chimneys, French windows, and enclosed gardens. In the Maxie family for many generations, the house is now the residence of Simon and Eleanor Maxie. With Simon dying in an upstairs bedroom (physically and mentally he has been little more than a vegetable the past three years), the management of Martingale rests in the very capable hands of his wife, a woman of serene gentility. Eleanor Maxie copes "with shattering common sense with those difficulties which were too obvious to ignore," and she ignores the rest (28).

In the opening scene, a prologue to the tragic events to follow, Mrs. Maxie is entertaining. Present at dinner are her two children: Stephen, a shallow, self-centered young doctor; and Deborah Riscoe, a widow of great composure and beauty. Also present are a weekend guest, Catherine Bowers, a dull young woman, who believes she is in love with Stephen; and three outsiders: Dr. Epps, a country practitioner, who serves the family's physical needs; Mr. Hinks, the vicar of Chadfleet, who serves their spiritual needs; and Miss Liddell, Warden of St. Mary's Refuge for Girls, who sees herself as Chadfleet's moral watchdog.

Waiting on them at table is Sally Jupp, an unwed mother, one of Miss Liddell's girls. Sally has assumed some of the household chores from Martha Bultitaft, the family's loyal retainer, most of whose time is now spent in caring for Mr. Maxie. A spirited discussion, not in Sally's presence, takes place on the subject of unwed mothers, with Stephen defending rather vigorously society's responsibility to them. Already, Sally is creating dissension among those at Martingale.

The next scene takes place three months later on the grounds of Martingale, the day of the annual church fete, complete with red and white marquees, stalls, a tea tent, and pony rides. Present in addition to the family and the guests from the earlier dinner are assorted town folk and Felix Hearne, a sophisticated and sardonic publisher in love with Deborah. He has looked forward to this weekend: "A house full of people all disliking each other is bound to be explosive" (32). Sally causes a stir by wearing a dress identical to Deborah's. But that contretemps is nothing compared to Sally's announcement at dinner that night in a voice "almost obsequious in its derisive respectfulness" (53) that Stephen has asked her to be his bride. The festive atmosphere abruptly ceases.

When Martha goes to Sally's room the next morning to find out why she is not yet in the kitchen, she finds the door locked; the only reply is the whimpering of Sally's baby, Jimmie. The household is summoned. When Felix and Stephen climb a ladder into her second story bedroom, they find her in bed, her flaming red hair spread over the pillow, her eyes closed, and a trickle of dried blood at the corner of her mouth. "On each side of her neck was a bruise where her killer's hands had choked the life from her" (59).

Who Killed Sally Jupp?

When Detective Chief-Inspector Adam Dalgliesh[3] and his assistant, Sergeant Martin, arrive from Scotland Yard to open the second phase of the drama, they find no lack of suspects. Catherine Bowers had reason to hate Sally for taking Stephen away; she had gone to Sally's room at midnight to talk to her, but at her knock she heard the bolt to the door being drawn. Mrs. Maxie strongly disapproved of the engagement, but as she tells Dalgliesh, "One does not kill to avoid social inconvenience" (96).

It is no secret that Deborah hated Sally; in fact, she wished her dead, as she had admitted to Felix. As for the old housekeeper, although Sally had been hired to help Martha, that relief had been a mixed blessing. Martha resented Sally and entertained pleasant fantasies of her dead. And although Stephen had no apparent motive, he grieved little for Sally. He has no idea what she thought of him. Although Felix appears to have no reason to kill Sally, since her marriage would drive Deborah from Martingale into his arms, still, if Deborah wanted her dead, he might kill to prove his love.

Difficult as it is to conceive of either the doctor or the vicar as a murderer, it is certainly possible to see Miss Liddell as a suspect. She had vented a spate of invective at Sally after her dramatic announcement, provoking Sally to call her a "sex-starved old hypocrite" and to threaten her with disclosure of some scandal (54).

Since Martingale was open to the public that day and since there was a convenient ladder to climb to Sally's room, the possibility even exists that an outsider is responsible. For example, there is the nervous looking stranger Deborah had encountered in the house that afternoon. Then there is Derek Pullen, a local lad, who had been meeting Sally surreptiously at night. There is also an unknown man that a young village boy, enjoying goodies and the comics in the privacy of a barn loft on the grounds, overheard the day of the fete arguing with Sally on the subject of money. All the youngster saw of the man was a gloved hand replacing the trap to the loft. Finally, there is Jimmy's unknown father.

As always in a murder investigation, there are a number of puzzling questions, the answers to which could lead to the killer. Why was Mrs. Maxie so sure Sally's door could not be locked? Why did Martha insist Sally must have killed herself? Who drugged the cup of cocoa found beside Sally's bed? Who stole the sleeping pills from the medicine chest after the body was discovered? Why did Sally tell the vicar two days before Stephen's proposal that Jimmie would soon have a father?

To answer the question, "Who killed Sally Jupp?" means first to answer the question, "Who was Sally Jupp?" The heart of any murder investigation is the victim. Dalgliesh will know the murderer when he knows the victim well.

"Cover Her Face"

When Stephen tells Felix after they have discovered Sally's body to "cover her face," he is referring, whether he knows it or not, to that celebrated line in John Webster's *The Duchess of Malfi* (1613–14).

In the play, Duke Ferdinand and the Cardinal, his brother, enraged that the duchess, their sister, has married her low-born steward and borne his children, hire the criminal Bosola to arrange her death and that of her children. Bosola and his executioners strangle them. Gazing at the sister he has sworn never to look at again, Ferdinand says, "Cover her face; mine eyes dazzle; she died young" (IV, ii). Though dead, she haunts the dark consciences of Bosola and Ferdinand.

As Dalgliesh investigates Sally's murder and uncovers her complex personality, he keeps her face fixed in his mind. In death Sally Jupp becomes a very real presence to him. As Robin W. Winks points out, the word *detect* as it is used in many detective stories still carries with it some of its older meanings: to lay bare, expose, "to discover a person being."[4] *Cover Her Face* is as much concerned with who Sally was—"to discover a person being"—as it is with who killed her and why.

Dalgliesh's investigation takes him from the drawing rooms of Martingale to the modest home of the Proctors, Sally's aunt and uncle who raised her after she was orphaned; to the Select Book Club in London, where she worked for a time; to the comfortable parlor of St. Mary's Refuge, where she went when pregnant; to Dr. Epps's pleasant Georgian home; to the Pullen's depressing cottage with its blue wallpaper dotted with pink stars. A portrait of Sally slowly emerges.

Sally liked to pretend, perhaps because she was so grudgingly raised by relatives. She liked to set up situations that she could control. She wanted power over those who, she felt, thought themselves her betters. She was a stage manager, but those whose lives she wished to direct were not characters in a play but men and women in real life.

At the Select Book Club, according to Miss Molpas, the director, Sally would ask for advice about her wardrobe, "as if she cared a damn" what others thought (200). Miss Molpas found her "too scheming" to end up an unwed mother (202). As it turns out, Sally was married. Her husband returns late in the book from South America, where he had been working. But because secrecy appealed to her, she told no one about her marriage. Believing society "salves its conscience more by helping the interestingly unfortunate than the dull deserving" (239), she passed herself off as an unwed mother to see what would happen. Mischievous as a child, she was manipulative as an adult.

Sally gave the impression of "meekness, respectfulness, and willingness to learn" (24); she seemed "a paragon of intelligence, capabil-
ity, and refinement" (29). She was a good mother and, on the
evidence of her letters to her husband, a loving wife. She was also
secretive, rash, and acquisitive. She was a clever liar, sly and scheming and deceitful, all the time laughing behind people's backs, getting a thrill out of wearing the same dress as Deborah Riscoe or using
her cocoa mug. She looked "positively triumphant" (116) when she
dropped her bombshell about the proposal, enjoying immensely the
Maxies' consternation "at a danger which only she knew had no reality" (239).

Stephen's proposal of marriage promised new excitement, another
opportunity to be secretive and mysterious, another chance to play
with people, to gain an upper hand, and combat what must have been
a deep feeling of insecurity on her part. The private joke, however,
backfired, and Sally's murderer took control of the situation. Now
this once vibrant woman is "destined for the pathologist's knife and
the analyst's bottle" (68).

"And the Murderer Is. . . ."

In a scene out of the classic detective stories of the 1920s, Dalgliesh gathers all the suspects together, and in his "calm deep voice"
(223) explains what happened at Martingale the night of the church
fete.

He first disposes of several red herrings including a clock that was
altered to establish an alibi and the unrelated crime of a drugged cup
of cocoa. He next explains how Sally was murdered in a room that
was locked from the inside. Through his powers of deduction and
from his observation of the lack of scratches on Sally's neck and
through the process of elimination by determining the comings
and goings of the various suspects, he arrives at the killer's identity.

As Eleanor Maxie puts it, "Think it out for yourself. Who else
could it have been" (248)?

She had gone to Sally's room to talk to her about the engagement.
But Sally was not a kind person. If she had not laughed at Mrs.
Maxie and deliberately lied to her when she said she was expecting
Stephen's baby, she might still be alive. One moment "she was alive
and laughing." The next second "she was a dead thing" in Mrs. Max-
ie's hands (248). All that kept Mrs. Maxie from immediately confess-

ing was her dying husband. She wanted him to die in peace. A few hours before Dalgliesh gathered his suspects, Simon Maxie died. There was no longer any need for her to keep silent.

Evaluation

Cover Her Face is a satisfying mystery. The clues are well laid out. When Dalgliesh first questions Mrs. Maxie, he notes her short nails, just as he has noted Deborah's long ones. When he hears about the man in the loft, he wonders why anyone would wear gloves in July. He knows of Mrs. Maxie's certainty that Sally's door could not be locked. He remembers her comment to him that "there must be a limit to what" people like Sally can expect (96).

At the same time, James has strewn enough red herrings to lead both the police and the reader astray as to who had access to the sleeping pills and the cocoa. There are other red herrings as well: Sir Reynold Price, a local Chadfleet bigwig, not only had access to the sleeping pills but had also visited the Select Book Club. Was he intent on adopting Jimmie Jupp because he was the child's father?

The clues are well planted, the red herrings well salted. Still, there are a few misgivings. Would the calm and serene Mrs. Maxie be so provoked as to strangle Sally? We are told that the police are swarming all over Martingale and Chadfleet, yet where is any evidence of police work other than the questioning of witnesses? The sudden appearance of Sally's husband and the unexpected arrival of Proctor, as well as the confession during the final scene, are stagy. So is the final scene itself, with the suspects gathered together waiting to learn which one of them is the murderer.

Style and Narrative Technique

In this, her first book, one notes certain characteristics in James's style and narrative technique common to all her novels.

Her books are leisurely paced. Certainly in *Cover Her Face* very little happens to propel the book forward, and in a mystery lack of action can be a failure. In her best work she substitutes for action exploration of character. But here, with the exception of Sally, we know little more about the characters at the end of the book than we do when we first meet them.

She can characterize with a pithy phrase or a witty sentence, reminding us here and elsewhere that Jane Austen is her favorite author. "Catherine Bowers is the sort of woman who tells her man that she will do anything for him, and sometimes does" (186). Miss Liddell keeps Dalgliesh waiting while she applies "powder to her face and resolution to her mind" (114).

James's ability to create a sense of place is a very real pleasure here and in the books to follow. Her interest in architecture is a passion she shares with Dalgliesh. Particularly fond of Georgian architecture, she includes a Georgian building in almost every one of her books. Dr. Epps in this book lives in a pleasant Georgian house. In her short story, "A Very Desirable Residence" (1977), a Georgian house even becomes a motive for a crime.

James takes great care in describing domestic interiors. Rose cottage with its ugly large plaster Alsatian dog occupying the front parlor window (170); Sally's bedroom with its plain anonymity; the comfortable, well-polished parlor of St. Mary's Refuge—all are highly individualized. One feels comfortably at home in them. That pleasure James finds in the interiors of Margery Allingham's and Dorothy L. Sayers's novels is one the reader can find in the settings of P. D. James.[5]

The narrative technique she employs in *Cover Her Face* is one she uses elsewhere. The novels are told in the third person, sometimes from the point of view of the omniscient author, sometimes from the point of view of a particular character. The ease with which she switches from one character's perspective to another's is testimony to her technical skills as a novelist. This ability also adds richness and variety to her plots.

Occasionally there is a problem when she enters the consciousness of her murderer; one wonders why the character gives not even a passing thought to his or her crime. For example, in *Cover Her Face*, we read Mrs. Maxie's thoughts about poor Sally, about Jimmie's future, and about her own problems in managing the house without Sally, but not one thought that a few hours ago she herself had killed Sally.

Adam Dalgliesh

The most notable aspect of *Cover Her Face* is its introduction of Adam Dalgliesh, the detective who appears in all but two of James's books.

More than anything else, Dalgliesh is a professional. In fact, he is so much a professional that his strong sense of compassion is hidden with the result that he appears almost distant, uninvolved. Patricia Craig sees his ability "to preserve detachment in the face of the aftermath of murder" as a "heroic quality."[6]

Dalgliesh takes his work seriously; and he is very good at his job. He brings to detection a solid grounding in police procedures, maintaining that a good policeman never theorizes "in advance of his facts" (68). He also possesses common sense, which is the basis of successful police work, the blessing of total recall, a sympathetic imagination, and shrewd intuition. Part of his reputation rests on his educated and successful hunches.

Dalgliesh profoundly believes that murder is an affront to society, that the health of society demands justice. He sees himself as an instrument—not a dispenser—of justice. He would like to tell Deborah that he is sorry he has to expose her mother as the murderer, but he can't say that because he isn't sorry; he would not insult her intelligence by pretending otherwise (254).

As he pursues an investigation he always keeps the victim fixed in his mind. Interestingly, in answer to whether he wishes to question the suspects, the very first words he utters are, "No, I'll see the body first. The living will keep" (62). No matter how despicable or deserving of dispatch, the victim has been unnaturally deprived of his or her span of years. This belief underlies all his investigations.

When he examines the body, he is never conscious of pity or anger. Although these emotions might show up later, a good policeman must resist them. He cannot allow himself to become emotionally involved in the lives of either victim or suspect. For a man careful to avoid commitment, Dalgliesh believes that detective work is the ideal job. Although he must constantly interfere in other people's lives, he must and does remain aloof from them.

Dalgliesh, however, does find emotional release in his poetry. He is not a detective who also happens to be a poet; it is because he is a detective that he is also a poet. Not until his second recorded case, *A Mind to Murder*, three years after the events of *Cover Her Face*, do we learn that his first book of poems is in its third printing and that it is published by Felix Hearne's firm. In a later book, *Death of an Expert Witness*, his assistant wonders what, if anything, can move the chief to pity. He then recalls a child-killing a year before. Dalgliesh had treated the parents with an almost calm detachment, working long hours until he cracked the case. There is included in his next book of poems an extraordinary one about a murdered child. And the title of one of his volumes, significantly, is *Invisible Scars*. In his passion for justice, Dalgliesh has the uncanny ability to ferret from those under question surprising facts and unpleasant admissions. "Pretty brutal" (78) is how Sergeant Martin characterizes Dalgliesh's questioning of suspects, but he also believes that if the witness being interrogated were the killer, "before long, he would see in Dalgliesh, patient, uncensorious, and omnipotent, the father confessor whom his conscience craved" (172). Never does Dalgliesh lose his temper with witnesses. Even Stephen Maxie, who thinks little of him, has nothing but praise for his handling of Sally's husband, James Ritchie. Although Dalgliesh never deliberately sets out to harm an individual, he knows that in doing his job, he cannot help but inflict pain at times.

Dalgliesh is also very human, and like most of us makes snap judgments about people. The moment Catherine Bowers walks into the room, he takes an instant dislike to her, just as he does to Elizabeth Marley in *Unnatural Causes* and Angela Foley in *Death of an Expert Witness*. He knows he is "prone to these personal antipathies," but he has "long ago learned both to conceal and evaluate them" (83).

James avoids giving a formal, full-length portrait of Dalgliesh. Unlike Hercule Poirot or Lord Peter Wimsey, he has few if any recognizable traits. Indeed, we know more about his mental states and feelings than we do his mannerisms. More often than not we see him through the eyes of others. Catherine Bowers finds him "tall, dark and handsome" with "an interesting face"; Stephen sees him as a "supercilious-looking devil." Felix has heard of his being "ruthless, unorthodox, working always against time," a man with "his own private compulsions." Mrs. Maxie wonders where she has seen his head before: "Of course. That Dürer. . . . Portrait of an Unknown Man" (73–74). Deborah feels that given different circumstances, "here was the man to whom she would have instinctively turned for reassurance and advice" (249). This indirect characterization no doubt accounts in part for Dalgliesh appearing to be somewhat distant.

From bits and pieces in the collected works, however, we do manage to learn a good deal about him. At the time of *Cover Her Face*, he is in his late thirties. Some eleven years earlier, his wife and only child, a son, died in childbirth. He has had affairs since and, as we learn in *Unnatural Causes*, he has had an intense relationship with

Deborah Riscoe three years after meeting her in *Cover Her Face*. Still, he uses his very genuine grief for his dead wife as an excuse for avoiding deep emotional attachments. Because of his personal tragedies, he "uses his job to save himself from involvement with other human beings."[7] James thinks it highly unlikely that he can ever "commit himself" again "to a lasting relationship."[8]

Dalgliesh lives alone in the nonresidential area of Queenhythe in London in a flat high above the Thames. In *Cover Her Face* he drives a Cooper Bristol, but by the time of *The Black Tower*, he has traded it for a Jensen Healey. He maintains a thirty-foot sailboat in an Essex estuary. He likes to eat simple English cooking, but often ignores meals when he is in the middle of a case. He finds no interest in those things that he cannot understand. Thus, although a clergyman's son, he does not or cannot believe in God. In the course of his books, he rises in rank from Detective Chief-Inspector to Commander.

In *Cover Her Face* Felix refers to him as a "cultured cop" (102) because he can identify a modern painting. As a matter of fact, Dalgliesh has an extensive knowledge of modern art and of architecture in general. When investigations or vacations take him outside London, he often packs one of the Newman and Pevsner guides to the buildings of England. He is a well-read man. Jane Austen and Thomas Hardy are his favorite authors; indeed, Austen's novels are always on his bedside table. He is not especially musical, contrapuntal being what he likes best. Bach and Vivaldi are his favorite composers.

He is, on the whole, a very private man, a loner, not easy to warm up to. At times, as in *Unnatural Causes*, he is downright testy; when he makes mistakes, he admits them. He is a fascinating and complex man, as three-dimensional a character as one will find in contemporary detective fiction.

Critical Reception

Anthony Boucher in the *New York Times* calls *Cover Her Face* "a literate and not unpromising first novel." At the same time, he complains that it is too firmly modeled on "the detective story of thirty years ago at its dullest," lacking plot as well as action. He had been waging a campaign for a return in mystery fiction to the formal detective story, but *Cover Her Face* was not what he meant.[9]

Barzun and Taylor in *A Catalogue of Crime* find the book "immensely pleasing and impressive."[10] That assessment is easy to agree with. The pace may be slow and the ingredients—the English country home setting, the locked room, the closed circle of suspects—conventional and traditional; still, the solution is logical, the writing impeccable, the sense of place well realized. The characterization of Sally Jupp, imaginative and power seeking, is life like. Best of all is the debut of Adam Dalgliesh.

James, herself, has a special fondness for the book. Because it is her first novel, she retains "for it that peculiarly defensive pride one has for a firstborn."[11] She need not be apologetic. *Cover Her Face* is more than a promising debut; it is the work of a mature writer.

Chapter Three
A Mind to Murder

P. D. James's second mystery, *A Mind to Murder* (London, 1963, New York, 1967),[1] represents an advance over *Cover Her Face*. The setting—the Steen Clinic, a psychiatric outpatient clinic in London—is a more contemporary and realistic one than the manor home of the first book. The setting allows James to anatomize unhappily married and unmarried men and women, the plight of many of her characters in this and subsequent books. The characters are more complex than those in *Cover Her Face* and like real men and women are full of surprises as they face the difficult problems of personal relationships.

A Mind to Murder is the first of her books to have a medical setting, the hallmark of her best mysteries. The use of such a setting reflects James's own experience as a hospital administrator and as a wife to a man incapacitated by mental illness. The medical setting also becomes a fit backdrop for one of James's most persistent themes—pain.

Pain is a key word in James. Characters suffer physical and mental pain. Victims die painfully; murderers kill out of a sense of pain. Cases are solved at the cost of pain to the suspects and detective alike. Pain in James's fiction is part of the human condition.

In *A Mind to Murder* one psychiatrist is himself in analysis because of his doomed marriage and unhappy divorce. Another doctor has seen both his marriage to a neurotic woman and his affair with his mistress end unhappily. His tired, dull eyes reflect his personal pain. The clinic's administrative officer has lost her mother, a suicide, to mental illness. Her cousin, a nurse at the clinic, cares for a mother incurably afflicted with multiple sclerosis, a favorite disease for James's characters. A hospital porter is aging and sick. A former patient, now cured, is exposed to further mental anguish when a blackmailer threatens to disclose his past. Dalgliesh, himself, relives the painful memory of the death years ago of his young wife and newborn son. At the end of the first night of the investigation he feels both a continuous throbbing pain and a lack of confidence (101). The successful conclusion to the case brings him no feeling of accomplishment and happiness but only a sense of personal gloom. As if to underscore the human unhappiness and insecurity that are the lot of her characters, James suffuses the book with an autumnal melancholy.

The Steen Clinic

The Steen Clinic is one of many structures in James that is being used for a purpose other than that originally intended. Formerly a stately Georgian private home, it now houses an outpatient clinic. In a mystery novel where situations and relationships are not always what they appear to be, a setting that likewise is not what it appears to be becomes an appropriate site for murder. The converted setting also reflects the fluid change that undermines the stability of society with the old inexorably making way for the new.

The Steen was founded by the family of Hyman Stein who suffered from impotence, received psychotherapy, and went on to sire children who anglicized their name and endowed a clinic in their father's name, likewise anglicized. The clinic has precariously maintained its independent status within the framework of the National Health Service. But once the murder is solved, further changes are in store. A rumor circulates that the Steen will be closed and the patients transferred to a hospital outpatient service.

James's picture of the clinic, its staff, and patients is gently satiric, reflecting her somewhat unsympathetic view of doctors. In *Cover Her Face*, James had already depicted an unpleasant doctor, Stephen Maxie, and in commenting on the medical profession's ability to prolong life, attributed the motive of these scientific miracle workers to self-esteem and personal glory.

The Steen has the reputation for dealing with only upper class neuroses, for choosing its patients on the basis of their social standing rather than on their state of mind (26). A witticism bandied about the clinic claims that one "had to be exceptionally sane to be accepted for treatment" (26).

Its well-trained, highly competent staff is jealously at odds with one another. A Freudian analyst carries on a childish rivalry over turf with a doctor who administers electro-convulsive therapy (ECT), "shocking his patients out of the few wits they still possessed" (12). Its administrative officer does not care for neurotics, taking out her resentment on the patients. A social worker "like many professional

social workers . . . had little instinctive understanding of people"
(103). The director of the clinic, a distinguished looking but shallow
man, devotes his energies "to making the profession respectable"
(25). James's view of the doctors at Steen can best be summed up
in the reaction to the doctors of a staff member's pet Pekinese:
"The company of more than one psychiatrist at a time made Hector
sick" (149).

Temperamental and contrary and insecure as these doctors may be,
as the secretary of the Hospital Management Committee, Mr. Lauder,
tells Dalgliesh, "I'd rather deal with a difficult psychiatrist than a difficult surgeon any day. They're the real *prima donnas*" (43).

Although the doctors lack alibis for the murder at Steen, the rest
of the staff cannot conceive of them as possible killers. No guts, according to Mrs. Shorthouse, the clinic's cleaning lady. Peter Nagle,
porter and budding artist, shares this sentiment: "They haven't the
nerve" (146).

Despite James's amusing portrayal of the Steen Clinic, sinister and
deadly happenings take place in its elegantly designed rooms. On a
Friday evening in October when the clinic is open late for private psychotherapy consultations, ECT sessions, and lysergic acid treatments,
Jennifer Priddy, a junior typist, on entering the basement records
room finds the medical files strewn over the floor. "And in the middle
of this confusion, like a plump and incongruous Ophelia afloat on a
tide of paper, was the body of Enid Bolam," administrative officer,
bashed over the head with a carved wooden statue, a fetish, and
stabbed through the heart with a black-handled chisel. "On her
chest" is the "heavy and grotesque" fetish. With "her hands folded
about its base," the virginal Miss Bolam "looked, horribly, like a parody of motherhood with her creature ritually laid to her breast" (17).

Dalgliesh's Dilemma

The murder at Steen saves Adam Dalgliesh—now Superintendent
Dalgliesh—from a perplexing decision. At the time of the murder he
is at the other end of the square from the Steen, attending the annual
sherry party his publisher is giving; his first book of poems had just
gone into its third printing. Also at the party is Deborah Riscoe,
whom he has not seen since the investigation of Sally Jupp's murder
three years earlier (*Cover Her Face*). At their last meeting, he thought
he might be in love with her. Yet if he now asks her to dinner and

she accepts, his solitary life will be threatened, a possibility that frightens him. Fortunately, he is called away by the murder at the Steen before he can act on his impulses.

The Murder of Miss Bolam

The one personality central to any murder investigation is the victim. It is essential for the detective to build a relationship with the dead person. Yet Dalgliesh knows, as he puts together the various impressions others have of the victim, that his final perception will be as distorted by prejudices and preconceptions as theirs.

Everyone who knew her agrees that Enid Bolam was a rigid, efficient woman who managed to put people's backs up. Her sense of morality left no doubts as to what was right and wrong. There was no room for moral equivocation. Formidable and humorless, she was also unimaginative and lonely, with little understanding of people. Willing to help them if they were in trouble, she could not enter into their feelings, nor did she wish to. Typical of her behavior was that she would buy food for the clinic cat, Tigger, but she would never pet it.

Her personal life, Dalgliesh discovers, was as efficient as her professional life, neat and obsessively tidy. Only some photos of her as a group leader of Girl Guides indicates a life apart from her work. Mr. Lauder sums up this pitiful life with the chilling comment that she never turned in an inaccurate report (44). Dalgliesh's equally bleak epitaph is that "she had a great sense of duty" (193).

Motives for Murder

On the surface, the case seems cut and dried. The obvious suspect with the obvious motive is Nurse Marion Bolam, Enid's cousin, who stands to inherit thirty thousand pounds, a sum that would ease her care of her mother. But Enid has told her cousin that she plans to disinherit her. "Here was the obvious motive, so understandable, so universal, so dear to any prosecuting counsel. Every juryman understood the lure of money" (52).

Marion had the motive, the opportunity, and the necessary medical knowledge to drive the chisel through her cousin's heart. But as the investigation continues, Dalgliesh senses the presence of an active intelligence equal to his behind the crime. "Most murders," he well knows, "are sordid little crimes bred out of ignorance and despair" (93), solved by common sense, the bedrock of all solid, successful police work. This murder appears to be the brainchild of a superior, if devious, intelligence. Dalgliesh does not believe that Marion possesses such intelligence.

Judging by the character and nature of the crime, conniving Peter Nagle is a suspect. The chisel is his; and the expertise with which it was used might well suggest the weapon's owner as the killer. Yet Nagle is one of the few suspects with an alibi. But for Dalgliesh, the fact that Nagle has an alibi is in itself suspect.

Then there is the question why, on the morning of the murder, Miss Bolam phoned Mr. Lauder to tell him something was going on at the clinic that had started before her time. She needed advice urgently. His reply that he would come around that evening could have been heard by any number of people who were covering the switchboard that day. That Miss Bolam had been killed because the murderer feared exposure seems plausible; that she had been killed for some other reason seems too much of a coincidence.

Dalgliesh believes that someone at Steen with access to the records is blackmailing former patients, who might fear disclosure of their problems to family, friends, or employers. He finds a blackmail victim, Colonel Fenton, who, each month as instructed, sends fifteen pounds to the administrative officer at Steen in an envelope addressed in green ink. The Colonel's wife had suddenly brought matters to a head by calling the clinic the day of the murder and giving Miss Bolam the details of the blackmail scheme.

Having found the motive, Dalgliesh knows the identity of the killer. One person alone checked and sorted the clinic mail. Afraid of exposure he could have summoned Bolam to the records room, strewn the floor with files, knowing that with her obsession for tidiness she would bend over to pick them up, struck her with the fetish, and then stabbed her. With his knowledge of anatomy from his art studies, Nagle would know where to strike.

Arriving at the clinic at night, Dalgliesh finds Nagle attempting to kill Jennifer Priddy, who has found out that his alibi is not sound. His arrival saves her. But Nagle, although admitting to blackmail, denies murdering Bolam; he accuses the detective of being overly clever. Moments later when Nurse Bolam arrives, Nagle grabs her bag, tosses it to Dalgliesh, and triumphantly tells him that in it he will find one hundred pounds, a first payment to Nagle to keep him quiet, along with a signed confession.

Obvious Suspect, Obvious Motive

"It was a perfectly straightforward case," Dalgliesh's superior tells him, "the obvious suspect, the obvious motive." But as Dalgliesh bleakly adds, "too obvious for me, apparently" (220). When Nagle entered the records room to steal Colonel Fenton's medical record and burn it, he not only saw Marion Bolam bending over her cousin's body, he also saw his opportunity. It was Nagle who placed the fetish on the body, a detail that misled Dalgliesh. It did not seem in character for Marion Bolam to add that scoffing touch.

It has been a humilitating experience for Dalgliesh. His superior tells him not to blame himself for concentrating on Nagle. Mrs. Shorthouse concludes that he did his best, "and there's no harm done to speak of." But "it was enough to taste this sour, corroding self-pity without enduring" his superior's moralizing and Mrs. Shorthouse's sympathies (223–24).

He needs a respite from crime and death. As he picks up the phone to call Deborah Riscoe, he rationalizes that a dinner invitation commits him to nothing. But as the next Dalgliesh mystery, *Unnatural Causes*, tells us, as a result of his call, he and Deborah become lovers.

The Fear of Failure

From the moment he enters the Steen clinic, Dalgliesh feels unsure of his own abilities. The split second timing of the murder and the mysterious placement of the wooden fetish convince him that he is being challenged by an intelligence that is a match to his own.

He has a compulsive need to solve a case as quickly as he can. His reputation rests not only on his solutions to murders but also on the pace of his investigations. Delay annoys him more than it does most people. The fact that this murder takes place at the start of a weekend only makes him more restless at possible delays.

At the beginning of the investigation, Dalgliesh is bothered by a "foreboding of tragedy and failure." The feeling is irrational; the case, after all, is still young, and his intelligence tells him "he was making progress" (182). He thinks he knows the motive, and "this is one of those rare cases in which knowing why is knowing who" (195).

He has never failed before and certainly will not now. Yet he can't rid himself of the nagging "fear that time was running out" (182). Even when the Fentons confirm his blackmail theory, "even at this

moment of imminent triumph," he has a sense of failure (184). As
he talks to Mrs. Fenton, nature seems to warn him. Dusk falls, a
smoldering bonfire fills "his nostrils with acrid smoke. The lawn was
a wet sponge under his feet" (184).

He attributes this feeling of doom to the season—autumn. Fourteen years earlier in another October his wife had died in childbirth.
The death of the year reminds him painfully of the death of the heart.

It is not the season alone that accounts for his failure; it is his
pride. His intelligence, his record, his impatience to solve the case,
his subconscious desire to find an adversary worthy of him lead him
to conclude that only an intelligent mind could be behind the murder. Nurse Bolam lacked that intelligence. He admits, moreover, "to
a perverse disposition" (98) to suspect the one man who was evidently
not even in the clinic at the time of the murder. To prove Peter
Nagle guilty is a challenge Superintendent Adam Dalgliesh cannot resist.

The Steen director's estimate of Dalgliesh is not far from the mark:
"He's obsessional and . . . he's intelligent." Then he astutely adds,
"That means that his mistakes will be the mistakes of an intelligent
man—always the most dangerous" (152).

A less intelligent and a less determined man might have settled for
the obvious, and in this case he would have been correct. When Sister
Ambrose, chief nurse, recounts the events at Steen that night to Be-
atrice Sharpe, the woman with whom she shares a semidetached,
Bea listens attentively. Neither "imaginative nor sensitive" (116),
Bea comes up with the right solution: Nurse Bolam is "probably their
first suspect already. She was on the spot; she hasn't an alibi. . . . "
Moreover, her medical knowledge would tell her "where to put that
chisel in." When Sister Ambrose tells her of the quarrel between the
cousins over the will, Bea is even more sure of Marion Bolam's guilt
(118).

The experience has been a sobering one for Dalgliesh. The one positive outcome of the case, as he sees it, is that if this case does not
cure him "of conceit, nothing will" (220).

By revealing Dalgliesh to be more fallible than a Hercule Poirot or
a Philo Vance, James makes her aloof detective more sympathetic,
more attractive. Not simply a logical thinking machine, rather, Dalgliesh is a man capable of being hoist on the petard of his own intelligence. In no other of his cases will he be as self-confident as he is
here.

The Rules of Murder

In 1928, S. S. Van Dine (Willard Huntington Wright), the creator of Philo Vance, set forth in the *American Magazine* a list of "Twenty Rules for Writing Detective Stories." Although many of the rules show their age, some are still valid. Along with the rule that servants and persons who have played a less than prominent part in the story should not turn out to be the murderer, Van Dine maintains that the culprit must be "one that wouldn't ordinarily come under suspicion."[2] Readers can justifiably complain if the "who" in "whodunit" is too obvious.

Van Dine would not have approved James making Nurse Bolam the murderer. She is the obvious suspect, something that James never lets us forget. Yet when we come to the book's final disclosure, we feel jolted and surprised. James has successfully led us down the garden path, deceiving us with a red herring of gigantic proportions.

In *Cover Her Face* the drugging of Sally Jupp is unrelated to her murder. In *A Mind to Murder* and *The Skull beneath the Skin* the crimes of blackmail and murder are unconnected. Yet for much of *A Mind to Murder*, we believe, as does Dalgliesh, that blackmail is the motive for murder. When he declares that Nagle is both blackmailer and murderer, the facts all fit, the solution is plausible. We are satisfied. So, when it turns out he is wrong, when we learn that Nurse Bolam is, indeed, the killer, we are genuinely and pleasantly surprised.

The surprise ending, the final twist, much favored by Agatha Christie, Ellery Queen, and, even at times by Van Dine, is not in itself a departure from the practice in the classical detective novel. That the obvious suspect turns out to be the murderer, however, is a startling departure, not only from Van Dine's rules, but also from what one has come to expect in detective fiction.

Christie and James

In defining the difference between herself and Agatha Christie, with whom she is often compared, James says that "I just don't think we're doing the same thing." In a Christie mystery, she continues, the characters are not real. "You don't feel . . . any particular sorrow for the victim and certainly no pity for the murderer." James points out that although some of her own characters may be "rather horrid," still, "many of them . . . are at the mercy of their own compulsions, their own unhappiness." They are real people who bleed real blood.[3]

In Agatha Christie's *Peril at End House* (1932), the murderer and her victim are cousins, just as the murderer and her victim are cousins in *A Mind to Murder*. In the Christie book, a baffling, intricate mystery with an ingenious solution, the reader feels little, if anything, for Nick Buckley and her cousin, Maggie, cardboard characters, who serve only as pieces in the puzzle. In James's book, "a perfectly straightforward case" (220) by contrast, the reader does feel that sympathy and sorrow James speaks of for Marion Bolam, who kills to provide for her invalid mother, and her cousin Enid, whose life is as bare as her spartan apartment. It is her ability to make the reader feel that way that sets her apart not only from Christie but also from most other practitioners in the field.

Evaluation

A Mind to Murder is well plotted, the clues are planted fairly, the questioning of suspects, as always in James, is intelligently and interestingly done, the investigation of leads is thorough and meticulous. The surprise ending makes the book more complex than her first mystery and more clever than several subsequent ones. The writing is literate. With a few witty words she can bring to life characters who are only a part of the background: waitresses in a coffee bar who "looked like *avant-garde* debutantes earning their pin money" (161).

Best of all is James's intimate, somewhat satiric picture of the Steen Clinic—its doctors, nurses, therapists, administrators, clerical help, and porters. Her inside knowledge of the British Hospital System through her work for the National Health Service gives the book its authenticity and authority.

James lets us see her characters operating under pressure—not only the pressure of a murderer in their midst, but also the daily pressures of their professional and personal lives. We watch the jockeying for position up the bureaucratic ladder, the internal rivalries, and the unhappy home lives of men and women dedicated to the service of the mentally ill. In such a society weakened by jealousies and strife and personal problems, the way is clear for a conscienceless man to blackmail and for an abject woman to murder.

Though they are caught, neither the blackmailer nor the murderer will be punished for their crimes. Nagle will go to jail not for blackmail—in order to spare the Fentons further mental anguish—nor for attempted murder—Priddy, hopelessly in love with him, will not testify against him—but for the lesser crime of accessory after the fact. Because of diminished responsibility, Marion Bolam will not stand trial, one of the few instances in James where a murderer does not pay for her crime with her life. Unlike most mysteries, *A Mind to Murder* does not end conclusively.

Dalgliesh feels no sense of triumph at the solution but only the humiliation of overweening self-confidence. He also feels a distaste for the image he projects, that of the "uninvolved, uncensorious inquisitor of other people's misery and guilt" (197). Yet to get involved could lessen his effectiveness as a detective. Still, he sympathizes with one doctor, "rejected by his mistress . . . in favor of a private happiness [her conversion to Catholicism] which he could neither share nor understand" (165). He finds dismal, indeed, the prospect of Priddy, despite Nagle's attempt to kill her, "planning their life together when he comes out" of jail. Dalgliesh sadly adds, "And God help her when he does" (222).

Critics have found the book better than *Cover Her Face*, mainly because of James's sure handling of the medical background, a far more original setting than the manor home of her first novel, the startling final twist, the accuracy of the social and psychological insights, and the melancholy tone that underlies the book.[4] James, herself, is fond of the book as proof that she was not a one-book writer.[5]

Although *A Mind to Murder* is not on the same level as *Shroud for a Nightingale* and *Death of an Expert Witness*, her best books, whose characterizations and exploration of themes are deeper, it certainly points in their direction.

Chapter Four
Unnatural Causes

Unnatural Causes (1967),[1] P. D. James's third mystery, shows some restlessness and impatience with the genre. Although a mystery and thriller, a good part of the book is also a parody of the classical mystery in general and the mystery novels of Dorothy L. Sayers in particular. In that parody is a form of literary compliment, *Unnatural Causes* does pay homage to a writer whose influence James has acknowledged. In that parody makes fun of what it is parodying, James is "putting some breathing space between herself and Sayers,"[2] as if to say that the world of Sayers is not the world of James, the world of post–World War II England.

Unnatural Causes is set on the English coast of Suffolk. She had always wanted to write about the Dunwich coast—where she had a vacation cottage—with "the sea slowly eating it away."[3] As in other of her mysteries, the setting underscores the inevitable change in contemporary England.

In this novel as in her other coastal mystery, *The Black Tower*, Dalgliesh is on vacation. This plot device provides variety to the series and lets us see Dalgliesh under less formal circumstances. Though on vacation, he can escape neither murder nor the pressure of personal problems.

Dalgliesh's Holiday

Adam Dalgliesh has come to Monksmere, a small village on the Suffolk coast, for a ten-day holiday at his aunt Jane's cottage, Pentlands. His spinster aunt, a respected amateur ornithologist, is his only living relative. The thought of sheets scented with woodsmoke, teas before a blazing fire, and desultory walks along the deserted beach offers a welcomed respite after the customary red tape of Scotland Yard and the investigation of a brutal child murder.

But there is more on Dalgliesh's mind than watching birds and taking leisurely strolls. His relationship with Deborah Riscoe has reached a moment of decision. They have been lovers for a year; now he must decide whether to ask her to marry him. Knowing her dislike, even her resentment, of his job, he is sure of her answer. At his aunt's he will have the time and the quiet to decide his future. "His aunt was the most detached, and incurious of women to whom the habits of birds had always appeared of greater interest than those of humans" (69). She is "sensitive, uncommunicative and rather difficult" (15), adjectives that apply to Dalgliesh as well. She makes "no demands on him, not even the demands of affection"; moreover, she is "the only woman in the world with whom he was completely at peace" (17). In Jane, Deborah has a serious rival for his affections.

Dalgliesh has been only a few hours into his holiday, however, when word comes that Maurice Seton, a member of the local literary set, has been found dead in the bottom of a dinghy, his hands severed at the wrists.

The Literary Colony

A second-rate writer of mysteries, Seton scores only second-rate as a human being. Dalgliesh saw him as a "pedantic, nervous and self-opinionated little man" (119), words echoed by Seton's publisher: "A precise, self-opinionated, nervous little man" (149). James's characters do tend to speak alike.

The doyenne of the Monksmere literary community is Celia Calthrop, who every six months turns out a romantic novel. Dalgliesh thought it "easy to be unkind" about "her reprehensible fiction" (73). She supports her niece, Elizabeth Marley, a student at Cambridge, an act of generosity that Celia does not let go unnoticed, any more than does Clarissa Lisle in a similar act of generosity in *The Skull beneath the Skin*. After the suicide of Seton's wife—driven to it, some say, by Seton—Celia had offered herself to him, only to be silently spurned.

Two other members of the literary community have reason to dislike Seton: Oliver Latham and Justin Bryce. Latham, a drama critic, had panned Maurice's one attempt at playwrighting. He had reasons other than bad dramaturgy, however, to hate Seton. He and Seton's wife had been lovers; in fact, he blames Maurice for her death.

Justin Bryce also blames Maurice for a death, that of his beloved Arabella, a cat. An inveterate gossip, an asthmatic, and a homosexual, Justin edits a conservative political and literary journal with book reviews of works "nobody wants to read" (52).

Of the other major characters—Elizabeth Marley; Digby Seton, Maurice's half-brother; and Sylvia Kedge—only Sylvia has literary connections. She is Seton's secretary—although according to Celia, more drudge than secretary. Crippled by illness, she might have been beautiful if it weren't for her ugly legs "braced into calipers" and her "masculine hands distorted by her crutches" (28).

Sylvia uses her disability to make others feel "uncomfortably aware of their own undeserved good health," and they resent her for it (28). But with Seton now dead, the others will vie for her services: "They all like the idea of having a private secretary on call for two bob a thousand words, carbons supplied" (71).

James's writers are more often caricatures of literary types than they are believable characters. They seem to have stepped out of the pages of a 1930s mystery novel, knowing exactly what is required of them. Dalgliesh is surprised at the readiness with which they supply information and establish alibis, as if they are accustomed to doing so (43). Their reactions and behavior could well have their counterparts in one of Maurice's own mystery stories. All the same, they are involved in a very grisly murder, one that leads to a second equally horrifying killing.

Death from Natural Causes

The obvious suspect in the death and mutilation of Maurice Seton is his half-brother, Digby, who stands to inherit 200,000 pounds. "No motive so gladdens" a policeman's heart, Dalgliesh informs aunt Jane, "as the prospect of gain" (67). Dalgliesh has obviously learned his lesson from Marion Bolam's murder of her cousin in *A Mind to Murder*.

But two solid facts stand in the way of an arrest and conviction. At the time of Maurice's death, Digby was in jail; moreover, the postmortem reveals that Maurice died from natural causes, a heart attack. Inspector Reckless, who heads the investigation, is satisfied; Dalgliesh is not.

Retracing Maurice's last days takes Dalgliesh to a tawdry strip joint in Soho, one of many cheap night clubs springing up with great frequency in London; to an exclusive men's club; and to a section of London—Carrington Mews—that is being transformed into a residential complex. Here Digby Seton had recently settled. As is true of other buildings in James, Digby's chi-chi town house started life as something else. The premises were once a driving school. Now, they are dedicated to a more dignified and utilitarian purpose, the relief of London's persistent housing shortage (170). But change in James is not always for the better. The converted cottages are dark, small, and expensive, and the entrance to the complex smells strongly of urine (170). In this up-to-date but vulgar cottage, indicative of the changing profile of London, Maurice Seton was murdered.

Compared to the grubby night club and the mean streets of Carrington Mews, the Cadaver Club in Bloomsbury is an aristocratic relic of an older and less hurried London society. A male bastion, it includes in its membership detective writers, criminologists, barristers, and judges. That it excludes some of the best crime writers now on the scene—women—has more to do with "the expense of putting in a second set of lavatories" (140) than with male chauvinism. Moreover, club members thought murder not a fit topic to discuss in the presence of women (241).

From the club steward, Dalgliesh learns that Seton always took the same ground floor room; his heart condition precluded his walking up stairs, and he had no confidence in the elevator. From Seton's publisher, a club member, he learns that Seton planned to disinherit Digby.

On his way back to Monksmere, Dalgliesh formulates a theory as to how the murder was committed. But before he can act on his hunches, a second murder occurs—*Unnatural Causes* is the first James novel with multiple murders—that of Digby Seton. His had not been an easy death. He is discovered on the beach, his knees "drawn up," his "head twisted upwards," the "glazed eyes" making "one last despairing effort to catch the light." In his death agony, "he had bitten his bottom lip almost in two" and "with torn and bleeding hands" stuffed dirt into his mouth in a desperate and "delirious" attempt at "coolness and water" (182).

That night as wind, rain, and flood batter the tiny cottages precariously balanced over the highest point of the headland, Dalgliesh checks on the helpless Sylvia. On the roof of her cottage, she turns on him and armed with her leg irons and crutches, tries to send him to his death. But a gust of wind tears at the roof, unbalances Sylvia, and she is swept to her death. Fortunately, she has left behind a taped confession. Fortunately, for without it Dalgliesh could not prove his hunch and completely unravel the mystery.

A Perfect Murder

James terms Maurice's murder "particularly ingenious,"[4] but most readers will find the solution overly complicated and far-fetched. Sylvia wanted Maurice's sizable fortune. Even more, she sought revenge on the man who never showed her the ordinary courtesies of life, never thought of her as a woman. To accomplish her plan, she needed Digby. The attraction of 200,000 pounds was a strong enough lure into her deadly web.

For Digby to inherit, Maurice's death had to seem natural, and Digby had to be married. For Sylvia to get the money, she had to marry Digby and then rid herself of him. The two thus secretly married. When Maurice confided to Sylvia that he had a recurring nightmare of being buried alive, that he suffered from claustrophobia, Sylvia had her means for murder. Digby bought a secondhand motorcycle; next he purchased a long side car; then he secured a London residence with privacy and access to a garage.

Maurice was lured to Digby's house where Digby knocked him out and stuffed him into the coffinlike side car, its lid nailed shut but with air holes for breathing. Digby then got himself arrested on a drunk charge. By the time he was released next morning, Maurice had died of fright. His "tell-tale hands with the knuckles torn to the bone where he had battered them against his coffin lid" were the only signs of foul play (233).

Sylvia had always planned to kill Digby; only with him dead could she collect the money. When she realized he was getting too clever, she was afraid he would kill her first.

Parody

The preposterousness of Sylvia's scheme suggests that James may be parodying the impossible and puzzling crimes so popular in detective fiction of the 1920s and 1930s. Certainly when she describes Maurice Seton's novels she is parodying the formal detective story of the golden age.

Dalgliesh doesn't really like detective novels, objecting to their lack of realism. If he had read one of Seton's he would be justified in his bias. Their cozy English village setting and class-conscious cast of characters, their absence of violence, and their strongly held belief that "murderers aren't gentlemen" (150) characterize not only a Seton mystery but also many from the golden age.

In a Seton mystery, as in a Dorothy L. Sayers or Agatha Christie, the obsequious police take a back seat to the amateur sleuth. That Seton shies away from dispatching victims by shooting them but was "very sound on toxicology" (150) reminds one of Agatha Christie's fondness for poison as an instrument of death.

The Honorable Martin Carruthers, Seton's fictional sleuth, an expert on "wine, women, heraldry, the landed gentry, esoteric poisons and the finer points of the minor Elizabethan poets" (100), is an exaggerated version of Sayers's Lord Peter Wimsey. But if a Seton mystery in situation and character brings to mind Sayers or Christie, Seton's style from the few examples James provides suggests that he was imitating—but doing so quite badly—the hard-boiled school of writing exemplified by Dashiell Hammett and Ross MacDonald.

James's parody is not confined to Seton's novels. If the Honorable Martin evokes memories of Lord Peter, then the title of James's book, *Unnatural Causes*, recalls the title of Sayers's 1927 mystery, *Unnatural Death*. There, the deaths of several women seem natural until Lord Peter is reminded of the workings of an air lock in a motorcycle feed pipe. That is the clue as to how natural death can be induced. The victims are murdered by injections of air into their arteries, causing what appear to be fatal heart attacks. In James's book the motorcycle is the instrument of what also seems to be a natural death. In the opening chapter of a 1923 Sayers novel, *Whose Body?*, a corpse is found in a bathtub with nothing on but a pair of pince-nez, as startling a discovery as that which opens *Unnatural Causes*.

The opening sentence of James's book is the same opening sentence of the thriller Maurice was working on: "The corpse without hands lay in the bottom of a small sailing dinghy drifting just within sight of the Suffolk coast" (11). Celia Calthrop, whose fiction Dalgliesh finds deplorable, suggested the sentence to Maurice. She believes novels should start with a grabber. This is not the only instance in the book of life imitating art—and very bad art at that. Seton's death occurs as a result of a ploy he often used in working up methods of murder for his own books.

All this indicates that James intended parody. Yet as Hanna Charney in *The Detective Novel of Manners* observes, death "transcends parody (as death always does)."[5] And the two murders in *Unnatural*

Causes are especially gruesome. Moreover, when Elizabeth Marley berates others for not showing grief over Maurice's death, she iterates a concern that James takes very seriously: no matter how despicable the murdered person may be, the victim is a human being deprived of the full extent of a natural life. Neither Marley nor James finds murder an occasion for amusement as do those at Monksmere (195). Finally, although Maurice is dead on the first page of the mystery, James succeeds in bringing the pitiful little man to life. As Charney writes, "Seton does step out of the frame of parody . . . just enough to let some light fall on certain features by which we all recognize other characters in the novel as well as ourselves."[6]

In the mysteries that follow *Unnatural Causes*, James will craft novels of detection whose emphases are on character, psychological probings, and dark implications. Her mysteries will move in the direction of straight fiction. Not until *The Skull beneath the Skin*, fifteen years later, will she again employ parody; and in that work it is not Sayers she parodies but herself.

Evaluation

A major weakness in *Unnatural Causes* is the way in which Dalgliesh correctly hits upon the means of murder. Even here James may be parodying the thinking-machine mentality and logic of such cerebral detectives as Baroness Orczy's The Old Man in the Corner or Jacques Futrelle's Professor Van Dusen, the Thinking Machine. It is difficult to see how Dalgliesh comes up with the key that Maurice suffered from claustrophobia. Further, that James resorts to the awkward device of a taped confession rather than an explanation from Dalgliesh suggests that she was aware of the problem of how he knows what he does.

There are other weaknesses as well. The involvement with gangsters and a strip club is an unnecessary complication, especially since James is ill at ease with the setting. To make a gangster a clergyman's son like Dalgliesh is a gratuitous bit, and not even a clergyman's son would use the word "armigerous" in a conversation with a stripper. James's letting the reader in on Sylvia's thoughts is a problem here as is letting us in on Mrs. Maxie's thoughts in *Cover Her Face*. In both cases there is no mention of the crime. Certainly Sylvia would at least once think about a murder she has so carefully planned and, so it seems, successfully brought off.

The story's climax on Sylvia's roof, with the sea sweeping in and flooding her cottage, is the kind of melodramatic excess James is never comfortable with. Yet, as Bernard Benstock points out, "Malevolent Nature in Suffolk" does mirror "the malevolent and malcontent natures" of those living at Monksmere.[7] Since there is no proof to convict and since justice must be served, there is the storm, the fall from the roof, and the taped confession. In *The Black Tower*, her other coastal novel, which is likewise Gothic and melodramatic, the killer makes a long confession before he, too, plunges to his death. Again, there is little or no evidence for a court of law.

Sylvia Kedge

Although most of the characters are little more than caricatures or stereotypes, Sylvia is an exception. In *The Black Tower* James offers sympathetic portraits of the physically handicapped; but there is little sympathy generated by this repellent, despicable woman. Monstrous though she is, James does enable us to understand this woman pained in body and mind. Because Sylvia believes herself ugly, abnormal, and sexless and because she continually draws attention to her helpless condition, others also see her as ugly, abnormal, and sexless. Knowing that such feelings are irrational and ignoble, they dislike Sylvia for making them feel this way.

The fact that Sylvia offends others with her deformity leads her to think that if she had lived in another time, she might have been burned at the stake as a witch. But offending others is not the real problem; Sylvia offends herself. "I offend myself Superintendent. I offend myself" (217). One cannot forgive her deeds; neither can one forget those chilling words.

Dalgliesh

In *Unnatural Causes* Dalgliesh is in the unusual position of seeing someone else in charge of the murder investigation, a situation he's not sure he's going to like. Moreover, he and Inspector Reckless take an instant dislike to each other: Reckless resents his presence; and Dalgliesh can barely disguise his contempt for the inspector. Dalgliesh seems intent on solving the crime as much to show Reckless up as to see justice carried out.

Adding to the strain and to his irascibility is his unresolved relationship with Deborah Riscoe. The naturally aloof Dalgliesh jealously guards his privacy; yet if he marries her, that cherished solitude will be gone.

Though he thinks of calling her when he is in London for the day, he does not. Back at Monksmere, he writes her a ten line "metaphysical conceit" (198), the only example of his poetry we ever see, along with a note expressing a longing to see her. But before he can mail them, she writes that she is taking a position in America. She can no longer wait for him "to make up his mind"; she can no longer live "on the periphery of his life" (236).

When a recluse novelist of some reputation who lives at Monksmere asks why he became a detective, Dalgliesh replies that the job lets him "indulge a curiosity about people." Sinclair, the novelist, counters by suggesting that in being a policeman, he has "a professional excuse for remaining uninvolved" (117). There is no room in Dalgliesh's life for Deborah. He burns the poem and his note. By taking no action at all, he lets her slip out of his life. He will continue to have casual affairs; and James will even tease readers in later books with the possibility of a romance between Cordelia Gray and Dalgliesh. But he will not commit himself to any woman again.

With *Unnatural Causes*, the cycle begun with *Cover Her Face* where Dalgliesh met Deborah Riscoe comes to an end. In her first three books, James lets us see the public side of Dalgliesh, the detached, composed man who lives by "forms, measured forms." She also makes us privy to her detective's changing moods, his introspection, his personal feelings.

That James with this book has written three novels about Dalgliesh and will write three more is evidence that she admires him or, at the very least, sympathizes with him. Certainly he reflects her views and attitudes. He also possesses many of the qualities she admires in a man.[8] With his detachment and desire for privacy, Dalgliesh engages us as a character. A lonely man whose young wife and infant son have died, he has built a wall around his emotions. His professionalism and self-control maintain this protective shell. James has not sentimentalized her hero; still, there is something romantic about this aloof man who so young has experienced tragedy. Indeed, Erlene Hubly sees in Dalgliesh many of the traits of the Byronic hero, the man of sensibility and sensitivity scarred by life's traumas.[9]

Dalgliesh's continued attraction for his creator and her readers is his complexity of character. He is human and recognizable at the same time that he is aloof and impenetrable. A solitary man in a lonely profession, he is constantly thrust into life's tragedies and confronted with evil. He remains uninvolved with the people his job brings him into contact; at the same time he sympathizes with and feels for their weaknesses and dilemmas. That he is a sensitive man who writes poetry comes as no surprise. The association of these disparate aspects of personality and their reconciliation in the one man make Dalgliesh fascinating as a fictional character.[10]

As Dalgliesh begins his holiday in *Unnatural Causes*, he confesses to himself that he hasn't much liked himself lately (15), an estimate the reader may well share. He does not appear in the most flattering light; he seems to be burning on a short fuse. But it is this portrait, warts and all, that makes Dalgliesh one of the most realistic and one of the most intriguing detectives in contemporary mystery fiction.

Chapter Five
Shroud for a Nightingale

Shroud for a Nightingale (1971)[1] is one of P. D. James's most reward-
ing novels both in its assured handling of a complicated plot and
large cast of characters and in its examination of several thought-pro-
voking themes: the dark legacies of the past, love and possessiveness,
the use and abuse of power. The book draws an analogy between the
events within the closed community of its hospital setting and the
larger world outside. The book succeeds both as a novel of murder
and detection and as a novel of serious intent. The title announces
this dual character. "Shroud" refers not only to the burial garments,
the winding sheets, used to wrap corpses, but also to concealment as
in the phrase "shrouded in mystery." Both connotations are, of
course, appropriate for a thriller. But "shrouded" also carries the con-
notation of complexity, duplicity. In *Shroud for a Nightingale*, motiva-
tions, personal relationships, and questions of right and wrong,
innocence and guilt, are themselves wrapped in shadows, shrouded in
ambiguity.

Murder at Nightingale House

For her setting James draws once more on the milieu she knew
best, the medical scene. A hospital, as she has written, is an ideal
setting for murder, "a mysterious but fascinating world of men and
women performing a great variety of necessary jobs from consultant
surgeon to ward cleaner." It is a setting "where the reader, like the
patient, feels vulnerability."[2] James places her action at Nightingale
House, a nurse's training school on the grounds of John Carpendar, a
provincial hospital in Heatheringfield on the Sussex-Hampshire
border.

Like the Steen Clinic, which was once a private residence, Nightingale House was originally a private home, a huge Victorian house
"castellated and ornate to the point of fancy" (16). Topped by immense turrets, it is a fit locale for a Gothic novel. The school is

named not after Florence Nightingale—things are never what they seem to be in a mystery—but after its former owner, a Victorian manufacturer convicted of torturing a young maidservant, who to escape hanged herself. Her ghost, witnesses attest, weeps after dark as it roams the grounds—one of many dark pages from the past that haunts the present in this book.

On the morning that the inspector of nurse training schools for the Grand Nursing Council, Muriel Beale, makes her annual visit to Nightingale House, someone pours corrosive acid into the warm milk that is part of a student demonstration on how to feed a patient by intra-gastric tube. The murder, one of the most horrifying in James, is graphically described. As the carbolic acid drips into the tube and then into the stomach of Nurse Heather Pearson, it burns her stomach out. Face contorted, lips foaming, body writhing in agony, Pearce dies a horrible death, all the time screaming "like a stuck whistle" (25).

Not until a second student nurse, Jo Fallon, dies under equally mysterious circumstances two weeks later is Adam Dalgliesh called in. Fallon's nightly whisky and lemon has been poisoned with nicotine extracted from rose spray, a nod on James's part to Agatha Christie, who used the same means of murder in *Murder in Three Acts* (1935).

The World of Nightingale House

Dalgliesh focuses his investigation on the nursing staff in charge of the student nurses: Matron Mary Taylor and Sisters Ethel Brumfett, Mavis Gearing, and Hilda Rolfe. All are middle-aged spinsters in the same profession, but each is sharply individualized: stupid dull Brumfett, diligently devoted to nursing and to her idol, Matron Mary Taylor; frustrated Gearing, whose false gaiety masks uncomfortably passionate feelings; intelligent Rolfe, a lesbian, bitter of what life has brought her; and Matron, a beautiful, efficient, and formidable woman.

Nurses and students not only work at Nightingale House; they live there as well. James makes us aware of the stultifying effect living in such a closed community can have on personal lives. Jealousies, sexual frustration, thwarted ambitions abound. So easy is it for those in such proximity to learn about each other's habits and secrets that the sis-

ters must resort to "small pettinesses and subterfuges" (122) to hold
on to their privacy. Nightingale House breeds neuroses.

The effects of this claustrophobic world can be seen in the student
nurses as well. Pearce was a priggish young woman, insufferably self-
righteous, a self-appointed moral watchdog, but not above a little
blackmail. In a closed community such as Nightingale House, it was
not too difficult to find something unsavory about everyone. Since
Fallon was older than the other students, she developed a reputation
for being cold and aloof. Nurse Pardoe, promiscuous and out to get
all she can, uses other students and sisters, even sleeping with Rolfe
if that will help her get ahead.

James uses this world of women to examine the various ways of
love—love between woman and woman and love between man and
woman. The love one woman may have for another ranges in this
book from the purely sexual and selfish to the possessive to the purely
innocent and happy. As an intelligent woman, Rolfe knows that in
her relationship with Pardoe, she is "wasting love on a promiscuous
. . . little cheat" (139). Smitten as she is, Rolfe can't help thinking
whether it is "selfish or presumptuous to hope that the one who took
knew the value of the gift" (139). Ethel Brumfett is completely dedicated to Matron. They take tea together, golf together, vacation together. Brumfett is Matron's "protector, adviser, confidante" (280).
But her admiring love is not reciprocated; what keeps the relationship
together is Brumfett's knowledge of Matron's past. What keeps Muriel Beale and her companion for twenty-five years, Angela Burrows,
together, is their mutual but unspoken admiration for each other, different though the two women are in all other respects. This essentially innocent, nonsexual relationship is the happiest one in the
book.

Certainly relationships between men and women do not bring
much happiness in *Shroud for a Nightingale*. Jo Fallon's engagement to
a spendthrift actor was abruptly terminated when he committed suicide because of his homosexuality. Her subsequent affair with his
brother, Stephen Courtney-Briggs, senior consultant surgeon at John
Carpendar, had come to an end; she had entered her most recent affair, that with a young writer, not out of love or kindness or protection but because she wanted to sleep with him. At the time of her
death she was pregnant.

Mavis Gearing conducts a clandestine affair with an unhappily married man who is destined to remain unhappily married. Nurse Goodale marries happily, we are led to suppose, but must choose between

marriage and a career. In James, marriage is often at the expense of one facet of a woman's life, her career.

Dalgliesh's investigation extends beyond the conclave of students and sisters. It reaches into all areas of the school and beyond. We listen to a nonstop monologue of a housekeeper, more concerned with who took the corrosive acid from the lavatory than the use it was put to. We encounter a pharmacist, Mavis's lover, who carries with him an air of obsessive discontent nurtured by disappointment and unpopularity (193). We find ourselves in the presence of the senior consultant surgeon, a man of immense ego who sees everything in terms only of himself. So arrogant is Courtney-Briggs that he could possibly get away with murder. James bears little liking for doctors in general—"ghoul" is how Dalgliesh characterizes a pathologist in the book—and surgeons in particular. In *A Mind to Murder*, she characterizes surgeons as the prima donnas of the medical profession. Here, she is equally critical. The words may be Rolfe's, but the sentiments are surely James's: "I've never yet met a successful surgeon who wasn't convinced that he ranked only one degree lower than Almighty God" (148).

The Solution

The solution to the murders at Nightingale House lies in the past in one of the most evil chapters of twentieth-century history—Nazi Germany. A dying patient at John Carpendar had recognized one of the nurses as a former accused war criminal, Irmgard Grobel, who had been acquitted of taking part in the killing of Jewish slave workers in a German concentration camp. Though technically innocent—she was acting in accordance with the regulations and laws of the time—can anyone who worked at a concentration camp be innocent? Grobel's attempts to live down the past led to a new identity—Mary Taylor. It also led to emotional blackmail from Brumfett whom Taylor, in a moment of weakness, had confided in.

Dettinger, the patient, had told Pearce he recognized one of the sisters as Grobel. When Pearce blackmails Brumfett, mistakenly believing it was she Dettinger had seen, Brumfett kills her to protect her beloved Mary Taylor. Fallon had to die also for she possessed knowledge that could lead to Grobel. In turn, Taylor kills Brumfett to free herself of Brumfett's "intolerable devotion" (280).

The horrors of the concentration camp, a place of pain and suffering, live on thirty years later at Nightingale House, where nurses are trained to alleviate pain and suffering. Murder is indeed a "contaminating" crime, as Dalgliesh on more than one occasion points out.

No corridor, no room, no corner of Nightingale House offers escape from an oppressive threatening air of evil, associated with the ghost that haunts the grounds and the stench of Nazi Germany. There is not much difference between the striving after power that dominates the world of Nightingale House, and results in blackmail and murder, and the acquisition of power that marked Hitler's Germany and resulted in the Nazi persecution and extermination of all who were a threat to the regime.

Power

In talking about a hospital as a fit locale for mysteries James refers to it as a "strongly hierarchical community with its own esoteric rules and conventions."[3] Greed for power—getting to the top of that hierarchy—and the use of rules as a shield against personal involvement and responsibility are two of James's most deeply felt concerns in *Shroud for a Nightingale*.

"If all power corrupts," writes James, "then a doctor who literally holds life and death in his hands, must be at particular risk."[4] Courtney-Briggs wants to wield even more power than he has already. "Latent power only imperfectly controlled" exudes from him (126). But he is only one of many characters in the book who strive to exercise power over someone else and to expand their own sphere of authority.

Brumfett and Pearce use their power to compensate for otherwise drab and inadequate lives—as was true of many who joined the Nazi Party or the SS. They do not seek the riches and fame power can buy. Brumfett wants only a room next to her idol, "the prestige of being known as the Matron's friend" (284); Pearce asks only for a few shillings for one of her favorite charities, ironically an organization to help victims of Fascist oppression. Yet both relish the control they have over others no less than Courtney-Briggs does. They find power no less gratifying than he does.

"The exercise of power is always pleasurable" (283). So posits Dalgliesh, a man not without considerable power himself. Certainly Pearce must have exulted when she believed she found out Grobel's new identity; now she had one of the sisters in her power. Brumfett may have killed twice to protect Matron; still, the murders put Matron in her power, tied to her now "indissolubly for life" (287).

Julia Pardoe exerts her sexual powers over Hilda Rolfe, who will do anything to keep Julia's affections. When Rolfe no longer serves a purpose, Pardoe will drop her. Mrs. Dettinger, who knows what her son saw at John Carpendar, enjoys the power she has over Sergeant Masterson when he seeks the information from her. She uses her momentary upper-hand to get him to take her to a tango contest: "It's the ball or nothing" (236).

Pleasurable though power may be, it can breed violence: Mrs. Dettinger's temporary hold over Masterson leads him to thoughts of murder; Pearce's power over Brumfett makes her Brumfett's victim; Brumfett's power over Matron makes her Taylor's victim. Power gives birth to murder, and murder in turn has the power to disrupt and contaminate the lives of all caught in its entangling web.

As the person in charge of the investigation, Dalgliesh is in a powerful position. When Courtney-Briggs bristles at a question from Dalgliesh as not being within the detective's purview, Dalgliesh replies simply that is for him to decide (130). Earlier he had admonished Rolfe when she protested that her private affairs were none of his business that it was not for her to tell him what questions to ask. He will carry on the investigation as he sees fit. Her retort that he is playing a dangerous game in which he makes up the rules as he goes along elicits no response from him (108–9).

Unlike others, Dalgliesh does not use his power to promote his own personal goals or satisfy his ego or to get out of unpleasant duties. He does not begrudge "time on jobs which some of his colleagues thought more appropriate to a detective constable" (228). He uses his power as a professional. He will not lie, he will not suppress evidence, he will not overlook relevant information. He will remain firm to the rules and regulations. But rules and regulations can be a two-edged sword. Accused Nazi war criminals used them as a defense, indeed, as a sanction, to commit their heinous crimes.

In the final conversation between Dalgliesh and Mary Taylor, James examines the ambiguous nature of rules and by extension the ambiguous nature of men who utilize them.

Adam Dalgliesh and Mary Taylor

Of all the women Dalgliesh meets in the course of his investigations and in his personal life, Mary Taylor is the only one other than aunt Jane whom he admires as well as likes. She is James's most fascinating and intriguing killer if only because Dalgliesh is drawn to her. At their first meeting he is taken by her unconventional beauty and serenity. So much does he enjoy his conversations with this woman, his intellectual equal, that he must remind himself he is on official duty. Solitary and aloof and possessed of inner self-esteem, Mary Taylor and Adam Dalgliesh are much alike.

Taylor is not unaware of this similarity. "You and I," she tells him, "are not so very different after all" (291). Both hide their uncertainties about life behind the "convenient shields" (291) of regulations, the nursing code in her case, Scotland Yard rules in his. For both, rules and regulations offer professional reasons for remaining uninvolved with people. If he were to accept Brumfett's confession, as Taylor asks him to, "for the truth . . . it is" (290), he would be violating the rules of his profession behind which he justifies his own noninvolvement and quiets nagging doubts about the absolute nature of guilt and innocence. To do what Taylor wants would mean giving up his job. And that, she says, he cannot do. What would he be without his job? She then answers her own question: "Vulnerable like the rest of us. You might even have to begin living and feeling like a human being" (290).

Their conversation echoes one that Dalgliesh has with the novelist, Sinclair, in *Unnatural Causes*. Sinclair suggests that Dalgliesh's job with its code of regulations protects the policeman's privacy and gives him a professional reason to stay uninvolved. But coming from a man who has been a recluse and whose last book was published over thirty years ago, Sinclair's words seem slightly ironic.

The effect here is different. Dalgliesh says that Taylor's words cannot touch him, but the scene ends with Matron, seeing Dalgliesh's weakness, helping him to his feet. The weakness is the result of a physical attack on him earlier that evening. But physical vulnerability might be an acknowledgment of human vulnerability. Only a short time before this conversation, Dalgliesh was stubbornly determined not to betray any loss of physical control, any diminution of power, any vulnerability to his sergeant (268). But now dissimulation, at least in front of Mary Taylor, no longer seems necessary. Her words have gotten to him.

When Taylor wonders in the course of this encounter how Dalgliesh could possibly understand how intolerable was Brumfett's devotion, Dalgliesh replies, if only to himself, that he understands because he knows himself (280). If he can read her mind, it is because he can read his own.

This recognition of a kindred soul has frightening implications. For if Mary Taylor, a woman after Dalgliesh's own heart, turns out to be a cold-blooded killer, then could not Adam Dalgliesh? Earlier, Sergeant Masterson as he listens to Mrs. Dettinger's babblings can see how even he, a policeman, could easily be driven to violence. "The silly face smashed into pulp. Blow on blow on blow" (247). Mrs. Dettinger in her way and Mary Taylor in hers cause these men of law to recognize a dark side of their own personalities.

Perhaps because of this self-knowledge, as Dalgliesh tries to find evidence to use against Matron—evidence that does not exist—he pursues "the case as if it were a personal vendetta, hating himself and her" (293). For as Erlene Hubly congently points out, Mary Taylor has made him see a side of himself he would prefer not to have uncovered.[5]

In an interview James says of detectives in contemporary mysteries that they "are becoming much more complicated." A detective may well have within him "the seeds of corruption." Because today's mystery writers are increasingly concerned in showing their detectives as human beings, "that part of his personality which is evil has to be shown." The old distinctions in detective fiction between "the good and the bad, the dark and the light" disappear.[6] At the same time, she is quick to point out that understanding this does not mean condoning wrongdoing: "I think there's a difference between the acknowledgment of a common humanity and a sentimentality about crime, which I don't personally share."[7]

With her fondness for Jane Austen, James must recall Darcy's words to Elizabeth Bennett at Netherfield in *Pride and Prejudice*: "There is, I believe, in every disposition a tendency to some particular evil, a natural defect, which not even the best education can overcome" (chap. 11). A theologian might call this feeling original sin. Like all men and women, Adam Dalgliesh and Mary Taylor are victims of original sin whose forms in daily life are as many as there are beings.

A Happy Ending

That murder mysteries end happily should come as no surprise. The wrongdoer has been caught, evil—at least for the moment—eradicated, and stability once more restored to society. That is the case, at first glance, with the conclusion of *Shroud for a Nightingale*. Ethel Brumfett and Mary Taylor have paid for their crimes with their lives. Nurse Dakers, the terrified student nurse of the opening chapters, has now found poise and authority. The Burt twins have graduated, Nurse Goodale has married, and the unhappy Rolfe has passed from the scene to find surcease for her unhappiness in Africa. Nightingale House, itself, is being torn down to make way for a new functional, efficient building. The January rain of the first chapter has given way to August sunshine. Here is a world that Muriel Beale on her next inspection can recognize: "Here was normality, sanity" (296). All's right with the world again. Yet the happy ending does not dispel the somber tone of the book. The solution finds Dalgliesh not triumphant but troubled. The razing of Nightingale House rids the grounds of the ghost but does not resolve personal dilemmas.

Nor is Taylor's suicide without questions. As is all too common in James, the guilty must pay with their lives. Mary Taylor kills herself presumably out of remorse with the same poison she used on Brumfett and which had been used on the prisoners in the concentration camp, a tidy bit of retributive justice. One might argue that it is not in her personality to take her life. But punished she must be, particularly since there is no evidence that could be brought before a court of law. Still, one agrees with Norma Siebenheller who rightly feels "that the story would have been a better one had the scales [of justice] been left somewhat awry."[8]

Taylor's suicide note to Dalgliesh expresses no regrets. She tells him she was not guilty of the war crime charges. Hers had been a useful life; killing Brumfett was best for the hospital, best for Brumfett, best for her (293). This is a letter of justification, not of contrition. She sees no guilt in what she has done. If conscience leads her to take her life, then the suicide note does little to bear this out.

Taylor characterizes Dalgliesh in her note "as the embodiment of the moral law" (293), but he is not a vindictive man. As Mary Taylor has paid for her crime—though she is not aware of having committed one—he burns the note.

Reception

With *Shroud for a Nightingale*, James broke into a major world market. The book earned her high praise. Robin W. Winks calls it her best book: "Here mood, pace, style and atmosphere are all in perfect balance." In the estimate of the *New York Times*, it would be "hard to overpraise" the book.[9] It won awards from both the British Crime Writers Association and the Mystery Writers of America.

The accolades are justified. *Shroud for a Nightingale* is the traditional British mystery at its best: substantial, cleverly plotted, unflagging in its suspense. In its richly layered atmosphere and character studies, in its examination of human relationships, and in its probing into the dark shadows of human behavior, *Shroud for a Nightingale* offers the same satisfactions of serious nongenre fiction.

Chapter Six
An Unsuitable Job
for a Woman

James's fifth mystery, *An Unsuitable Job for a Woman* (1973),[1] features as detective Cordelia Gray, every bit as three-dimensional a character as Adam Dalgliesh. But he is certainly not absent from the book; his physical appearance is limited to the closing chapter, but his presence is felt throughout. Still, this is very much Cordelia's book, told, with the exception of a brief scene at the end, entirely from her consciousness.

James did have misgivings as to whether Dalgliesh fans would accept Cordelia. But she need not have worried. On the basis of this one book, Cordelia won her own dedicated following. Lillian de la Torre, past president of the Mystery Writers of America, wanted to adopt Cordelia.[2] And with good reason. She is James's most engaging and endearing character.

Writing about Cordelia presented James with fewer problems than writing about Dalgliesh. That she is a woman made it easier for James "to empathize with her situation." Since Cordelia is just starting out as a detective, James can show "her learning her job as she goes." With Dalgliesh she has to worry about his behaving like a Scotland Yard detective. To make him interesting, she has "to involve him more in detection and less in deskwork."[3] There are no such worries with Cordelia.

Cordelia Gray

Cordelia, spunky, slight of body, determined of will, savvy of mind, is "a real, true-blue, one-hundred-per cent heroine."[4] She is frail and tough, aggressive and vulnerable in equally impressive doses. Cordelia is not a beautiful woman: "a cat's face" is how she describes her own features (20). All of twenty-two, she seems more like a teenager being interviewed for her first job. What she lacks in physical strength, she more than makes up for in sharp wits and intelligence. Her nosiness, determination, and fearlessness serve her well in a profession many hold as unsuitable for a woman. She takes to heart the advice Bernie Pryde, her partner, has given her: You can't do our job . . . and be a gentleman" (91).

Shunted as a child from one foster home to another, Cordelia soon "learned that to show unhappiness was to risk the loss of love" (20). She remembers only one of her foster mothers with any affection. As a result, she has learned to fall back on her own resources. Withdrawing into self as a child, she has emerged as a supremely self-reliant and very sensitive woman. She knows what to make of what she sees, and she knows her own capabilities. Dalgliesh observes of her, "I don't think that young woman deludes herself about anything" (215). Being a private detective suits her.

At a convent school (though she is not a Catholic) she spent "the six most settled and happy years of her life, insulated by order and ceremony from the mess and muddle of life outside" (68). Thoughts of attending Cambridge were dashed when her father, "an itinerant Marxist poet and an amateur revolutionary" (28), who had stayed pretty much out of her life, summoned her. Then began her gypsy existence "as cook, nurse, messenger and general camp follower to Daddy and the comrades" (69). Like her namesake, Lear's loyal daughter, "What shall Cordelia speak? Love and be silent" (I, 1).

After her father's death, Cordelia took a job with a secretarial agency and was placed in Pryde's Detective Agency—"We take a Pride in our Work" (14)—as general factotum.

Bernie Pryde, a former policeman under Dalgliesh, let Cordelia help with one or two cases, and only two months before the action of *An Unsuitable Job for a Woman*, made her a partner. Financially, it was cheaper to let her take a share of the profits than to pay her a salary. Bernie is always extolling the virtues and methods of Dalgliesh; and he constantly quotes him. Although Cordelia suspects Bernie is quoting his own philosophy, she keeps in mind during her investigation of the case "what . . . the Super always said" (35): "Get to know the dead person. . . . Dead men can talk. They can lead you directly to their murderer" (37); "When you're examining a building look at it as you would a country church. . . . Ask yourself what you saw, not what you expected to see or what you hoped to see, but what you saw" (56); "Never tell an unnecessary lie; the truth has great authority" (188–89).

Fired from the C. I. D., Bernie is no more successful as a private detective. Neither he nor the agency were going anywhere. If he is a born loser, Cordelia is a sure winner. Little daunts her. She brings to the agency no particular qualifications or experience. But she is comfortable with others and with herself; people warm up to her, confide in her, certainly valuable assets for a detective. Without the cynicism or weariness one associates with the hard-boiled American private detective, such as Sam Spade or Lew Archer, she is disconcertingly honest; but Cordelia is also vulnerable, more so than Dalgliesh. James sees her as far "more aware of her own limitations" than he is of his.[5] That does not mean, however, that she can be easily taken advantage of.

Because Dalgliesh is responsible for Bernie's dismissal from the force, Cordelia thinks the Superintendent "supercilious, superior, sarcastic" (16). As it turns out, she and Dalgliesh share much in common: a love for Jane Austen and Thomas Hardy, a keen eye for works of art, a penchant for poking around country churches.

As detectives, both back up their hunches, but neither will theorize in advance of the facts (35). Both bring to their work clear heads, carefully considered lines of action, patient persistence, and moral indignation at crime. Both are very concerned with doing their jobs thoroughly, though neither is infallible. And in a tight situation, neither panics. Although they find themselves in the position of adversaries at their first encounter, Dalgliesh pays Cordelia a compliment: He acknowledges that she conducted the investigation as he himself would have.

In one other significant way are they alike. Both are very private people and, as such, they are bothered that their jobs require them to pry into the lives and affairs of others. Cordelia guards her privacy to such a degree, as we learn in *The Skull beneath the Skin* (1982), her second case, that none of her friends or colleagues have ever been in her flat. Neither of the two is by nature gregarious. A good detective must stand apart, separate from those he or she is investigating.

Cordelia's feelings about attachments are best seen in her attitude toward sexual relationships. She has no deep feelings for either of the two men she has slept with. Lovemaking, she decides, is "overrated. . . . the alienation between thought and action was so complete" (87).

In both career and life-threatening situations, Cordelia remains calm, almost detaching herself from the situation in order to analyze it dispassionately. Here again, as with the thought of love and the making of love, the separation between thought and action is complete. Interestingly, then, the one person in the novel she does become involved with in a strange kind of love affair is the dead boy whose death she is investigating. She is warned that it is risky "to become too personally involved with another human being," especially when that person is dead (55). Yet it is only through her emotional involvement and identification with the victim that she solves the case.

Death by Suicide

Of the six deaths in *An Unsuitable Job for a Woman*, three are officially designated as suicides and a fourth might well be. But it is only the first that raises no questions. Suffering from terminal cancer, Bernie Pryde takes his life, leaving the detective agency to Cordelia. Not that it is much of an inheritance. On the morning of Bernie's death, there are no clients, no cases, no appointments. Prospective clients would probably agree with a local bartender, herself a woman, that detective work "isn't a suitable job for a woman" (19). Still, Cordelia is determined to keep the business going until she can no longer pay the rent.

Relief comes when Sir Ronald Callender asks her to determine why his son Mark, a twenty-one-year-old dropout from Cambridge, took his own life. Cordelia sets out on her first real case with evident enjoyment: "Driving in happy anticipation through the sunbathed countryside . . . she was filled with the euphoria of hope" (44).

As Cordelia begins probing into Mark's life, she finds herself identifying with the youth. They are both the same age. Cordelia's mother had died in childbirth, Mark's a few months after his birth. Both had lonely childhoods, neither seeing much of their fathers; both are very private people. Offered the use of Mark's cottage by his former employers, the Marklands, Cordelia begins to wear Mark's sweater, reads his books, completes some gardening he had started, and sleeps in his bed. When she speaks to Mark's tutor, she hopes to hear that Mark was going to receive a First at Cambridge. When she finds a photo of a nude woman in the weeds outside the cottage, she feels dirtied. She is aware she is becoming too "sentimentally obsessed" with him (57). Perhaps her conviction that he was murdered is fueled by her desire to become his avenger.

The Investigation

Unlike Dalgliesh's cases which are restricted to a closed community, Cordelia's investigation takes her all over Cambridge and environs and far beyond. She attends a formal dinner party in Sir Ronald's Georgian home—like other old buildings in James, there have been changes; in this instance, the stable block has been converted to "functional but attractive" laboratories (31). She enjoys a lazy punt on the Cam and at a noisy student party she is "intrigued by the overt sexuality" (102). She visits a country graveyard to meet Mark's mother's former nanny; and in the garden of a house in Bury St. Edmunds she futilely tries to elicit information from the Callender's senile family doctor. She spends a day in London at Somerset House examining the contents of Mark's grandfather's will.

The investigation takes her back in time to the months before Mark was born. Ronald and Evelyn Callender had conspired with Ronald's mistress and secretary, Elizabeth Leaming, to defraud Evelyn's wealthy father into believing that Elizabeth's child by Ronald was his grandson and heir. When Mark learned of his true identity, his father—now Sir Ronald—murdered him to prevent disclosure of the deceit. Dressing his son in a black bra and lace panties and painting his lips purple, he made Mark appear as a sexual deviant who had accidentally hanged himself. Leaming had come across the body, redressed it, and wrote the suicide note.

As Cordelia gets closer to the truth, she is attacked by Sir Ronald's taciturn young assistant, Lunn, who throws her into an abandoned well where years before Miss Markland's illegitimate child had accidentally drowned. With Miss Markland's help and with the aid of a belt buckle belonging to another illegitimate child, Mark Callender, Cordelia inches her way up the well's stone wall to safety.

Of all the surprising and shocking revelations in the book, none is more surprising and shocking than Cordelia's complicity in Leaming's murder of Sir Ronald when Leaming learns the truth about Mark's death.

The Cover-Up

Considering Dalgliesh's refusal in *Shroud for a Nightingale* to suppress evidence, Cordelia's tampering with evidence to make it look as if Sir Ronald in a fit of depression killed himself comes as something of a jolt. Unlike Dalgliesh, who punctiliously heeds the rules, Cordelia is young and with youth comes idealism and a refusal to submit to the system. Called into the case by Sir Ronald's friends, unsatisfied at the official verdict of suicide, Dalgliesh believes Cordelia is lying out of "love, fear, or a sense of justice" (207). Certainly she is acting out of a moral, not a legal, concept of justice. With Sir Ronald's death, legal justice has been served. What could be accomplished by Leaming's trial except to bring to public attention the sordid facts of Mark's death. She does not think that is what Mark would want (174). It would make no difference to her if Leaming went to prison; she does not particularly like her. But she does not want to see Mark's mother sent to prison (179). Willing to sacrifice her career and integrity for Mark, Cordelia lies at the coroner's inquest. In learning as a child to keep her feelings to herself, Cordelia educated herself in the art of concealment. Subsequent deceits, she found, had been easy.

There is also a certain degree of female solidarity in Cordelia's action. She and Leaming have struck a blow against male dominance and superiority. As they await the police, Leaming asks, "What is there to be frightened of? We shall be dealing only with men" (180). All that she and Leaming have in common are their feelings for Mark and their sex. In the days following the cover-up, Cordelia begins to appreciate "the strength of that female allegiance" (200). James does consider herself to be a "tremendous feminist," although she disavows sympathy with the more extreme faction of women's liberation.[6] Women, she feels, are as intelligent as men, if not more so. Certainly Cordelia has outsmarted Sir Ronald, who would not have hired her if he thought she would uncover his duplicity. She has gotten the better of the police, and in her difficult confrontation with Dalgliesh, she does not flinch, although for the first time since the cover-up she becomes "desperately afraid" (210).

What before seemed fidelity to an abstract sense of moral duty now takes on deadly seriousness. If she is forced or persuaded or tricked into telling the truth, she could end up in jail as an accessory to murder. Interestingly, Cordelia's first thought on that prospect is not the loss of her license and livelihood but that prison stank and that her clothes would be taken from her. No longer the tough, independent woman, she becomes a frightened child. Dalgliesh, whom Bernie always looked up to, takes over from the dead Bernie the role of substitute father: Dalgliesh, the stern upholder of law, Cordelia, the willful, disobedient child.

For Cordelia to initiate her career as private detective under a cloud of lies and with the guilty knowledge of being an accessory to murder has fascinating implications for her future. To speculate on them, however, is academic, for James completely takes Cordelia off the hook on which she has temporarily put her. The uncomfortable interview with Dalgliesh abruptly stops with the news that Leaming has been killed in an automobile accident—or perhaps it was suicide— another fortuitous instance in James of retributive justice. Crime cannot go unpunished. James can allow Cordelia to conceal facts and suppress evidence for she knows all along that Leaming will die, justice be served, and Cordelia's reputation assured—and no one will be undeservedly harmed in the process.

Although Dalgliesh is positive that Cordelia knows the truth of the crime, he is equally positive that "she's proof against any interrogation" of his. That she is lying, he has no doubts; that she is "absolutely without guilt," he equally has no doubts (215). Perhaps he is getting older or more philosophical, but he consoles himself with the knowledge that "there are some crimes which are better left unsolved" (216).

Critics have questioned Cordelia's motives in these chapters and have complained that the pat ending, Leaming's death, spoils an otherwise fine mystery.[7] Some years after the book's publication, James did agree that Leaming was disposed of a bit too neatly. But she justifies Leaming's off-stage demise by claiming that "writers and readers require some kind of retribution" in crime fiction; that "if the murderer isn't to be hanged"—and the death penalty no longer exists in England—"then he's got to be rid of somehow."[8]

As Cordelia leaves Dalgliesh's office, free and safe, she bursts into tears of relief; she is glad to be leaving "this horrible place" (213)— like a naughty child locked in the woodshed. Dalgliesh, in turn, is glad that he will not be meeting her again, for in questioning her, he felt as if he were "corrupting the young" (215). Yet their farewell smiles suggest that at another time and under different conditions, they would not mind seeing each other.

Readers have hoped that would be the case. There are suggestions in The Black Tower, the next Dalgliesh mystery, that they might get involved. But by Death of an Expert Witness, such hopes have come to naught. James thinks it "highly doubtful" if Dalgliesh would ever commit himself to a lasting relationship, though she does not close the door to it. How a character like Dalgliesh develops, she confesses, is often outside his creator's understanding and control.[9]

In an article, "Ought Adam to Marry Cordelia," James points to those mysteries in which "the love interest complicates and confuses both the investigation and the hero's emotions," Ngaio Marsh's *Artists in Crime* (1937) and Dorothy L. Sayers's *Strong Poison* (1930). James does mention several famous husband and wife teams who work well together—Nick and Nora Charles, Pam and Jerry North, Tuppence and Tommy Beresford—although all these couples were married before their first appearance in a book. [10]

Certainly Adam and Cordelia would be aware of the weighty arguments against marriage; they are both highly intelligent people. "But then," James concludes, "when have two people married on the basis of prudence?" [11] Still, to marry them off "would be too pat. . . . And on a technical level, it would be very difficult to bring them together without having their relationship usurp the main action of the book." [12] The possibility of a relationship exists, but with each passing year—and it is now over ten years since they met—the sound of wedding bells grows even dimmer.

Victim and Killer

In mystery fiction in general and in the novels of P. D. James in particular, it is often difficult to find a kind word to say about victims. At times they seem to be asking to be murdered. Sally Jupp's taunts in *Cover Her Face* and Clarissa Lisle's malicious laughter in *The Skull beneath the Skin* invite murder as do Enid Bolam's disclosure to her cousin in *A Mind to Murder* that she is to be disinherited and Heather Pearce's blackmail threats in *Shroud for a Nightingale*.

With the saintly Mark Callender, however, we have something new in James, a victim who is a completely likable young man, the first James victim for whom we feel genuine grief and sorrow. Mark's friends remember him as being innately kind, sweet, gentle. He cared about people. He responded positively to children and they to him. With one uncontrollably wild autistic child, he worked wonders, sitting with him for hours, rocking him back and forth (88). He volunteered to sit with the senile Dr. Gladwin, a man he had never met before, to give the doctor's wife a brief respite.

In the short time he worked for the Marklands, he "created a little oasis of order and beauty out of chaos and neglect" (51). He wanted to make the world a better place; and he died because he could not bear to live with the lies and deceits of a disorderly world.

The close relationship that Cordelia develops with the dead Mark gives the book an added emotional dimension often lacking in detective fiction.

If James's victims are so often disagreeable, her killers, on the other hand, evoke sympathy and pity from the reader. Who can blame the murderers in *Cover Her Face* and *The Skull beneath the Skin* from striking out at their tormentors? Who does not sympathize with Elizabeth Leaming when she kills the man who murdered their son and tried to make him look like a sexual deviant? But it is impossible to feel any pity or sorrow for Sir Ronald Callender, James's most horrific killer.

At convent school, Cordelia had prayed daily, "Deliver us from evil." Now, as she accuses Sir Ronald of murder, she looks into his eyes and comes face to face with evil. If she had not believed in its existence before, she does now. He is a modern day variant of the "mad scientist," complete with his evil servant, Lunn. Though Sir Ronald desperately wanted a son, he cared more for Chris Lunn than for Mark. Not for Sir Ronald is Lord Byron's line, "Sweet to the father is his first born's birth." He had found Lunn in an orphanage, raised him, and trained him as his assistant. He has no regrets at the murder of his son, no remorse. He is convinced that Mark's death has served a purpose. To continue with his scientific work is worth at least one human life, even if that life is his son's and even if he is the man who has taken it. Like the moral monsters in the fiction of Nathaniel Hawthorne, he puts the head, the pursuit of an intellectual goal, over the heart, a commitment to human emotion.

James, Sayers, and MacDonald

Writers on P. D. James have often pointed out that in her sound plotting and careful construction, her lovingly described backgrounds—both Cordelia and the reader are bewitched by the pleasures of Cambridge in the summer so delightfully evoked—her considerable insight into character, and the satisfaction of her prose, she writes in the tradition of Dorothy L. Sayers. Nowhere is this better seen than in *An Unsuitable Job for a Woman*. Cordelia Gray at Cambridge cannot but help to bring to mind Harriet Vane at Oxford in Sayers's *Gaudy Night* (1932).

In an article on Sayers's influence, S. L. Clark points to specific parallels. Clark's thesis, well-supported, is that James's Cambridge novel "is designed to be a reshaping and redrawing of some of the concerns expressed by Sayers in *Gaudy Night*."[13] In *Unnatural Causes* James borrowed from Sayers to parody the classical detective mystery. In *An Unsuitable Job for a Woman* she duplicates certain superficialities in the situation and characters of *Gaudy Night*. James also takes up some of the same thematic concerns that preoccupied Sayers: the role of women in society, the question of individual responsibility, parent-child relations, the effects of the past on the present.[14] But now her object is not to parody but to look at these situations and concerns in a contemporary setting. In *Gaudy Night* Harriet Vane has to call in Lord Peter Wimsey for help. But the damsel in distress of the 1930s has given way in the 1970s to the plucky, self-confident woman. Not only does Cordelia not call for help, but she confronts the murderer all alone.

Yet when one talks about the effects of the past on the present with reference to *An Unsuitable Job for a Woman*, one is just as likely to think of Ross MacDonald, creator of Lew Archer, as of Sayers. In an Archer mystery what starts out to be a simple investigation turns into a complicated excursion into the past. In the Archer mysteries, a crime committed in the past leads to another crime years later. To solve the latter entails opening the earlier case with all its dark secrets. Often the original crime involves family secrets, tangled sexual relationships, and elaborately plotted lies and deceits. Many Archer stories are concerned with parents searching for lost children or children for lost parents.

The trail Cordelia pursues is always in Mark's footsteps as he searches for the truth of his parentage, a theme James returns to in *Innocent Blood* and the short story, "The Girl Who Loved Graveyards" (1984). If it is true, as James has said, that the hub of *An Unsuitable Job for a Woman* is Cordelia's relationship with Pryde's Detective Agency and its founder and owner, Bernie Pryde,[15] then Cordelia too might be looking for a lost father—her own dies soon after he reenters her life and Bernie commits suicide—whom she finds in the kind, courteous, and patient Dalgliesh.

The convoluted relationships and twists of plot of *An Unsuitable Job for a Woman* sound much like a description of a Lew Archer novel. A husband, his wife, and his mistress conspire to deceive the wife's father to ensure his fortune; the husband and his mistress hasten the wife's death by providing her with inadequate medical help; the husband pays more attention to an orphan whom he raises than to his natural son. Years later he murders the son, who has learned the truth of his parentage. On the night of the murder the mistress is in bed with the orphan. Later she murders the husband. Both she and the orphan die in automobile accidents. Two of these five deaths are murders made to look like suicides; a third might be a suicide made to look like an accident; a fourth may have been a murder made to look like a natural death.

James has paid tribute to the keen and perceptive understanding of California life and mores to be found in the novels of Ross MacDonald.[16] Certainly, as Clark proves, James's 1973 mystery "builds securely on a foundation" set by Sayers's 1935 mystery.[17] But equally certain is the influence on James of writers of the hard-boiled school like MacDonald and even Dashiell Hammett. Interestingly, in two of Hammett's novels, *Red Harvest* (1929) and *The Glass Key* (1931), the central crime is a murder of a son by his father, "a theme unusual in literature," according to Hammett's biographer, Diane Johnson.[18]

Whatever the influence of Sayers and MacDonald, there is no doubt that *An Unsuitable Job for a Woman* is a literate, intelligent, stylishly written detective novel. Nor is there any doubt that Cordelia Gray is a convincing picture both of a first-rate detective and a modern young woman. James may well have committed "the cardinal sin of falling in love with her great detective,"[19] but if she did, so did most reviewers and readers who hoped this novel would be the first of a series. But almost ten years went by before the next Cordelia Gray mystery. Perhaps James never meant Cordelia to be a series character. Whether she did or not, what is important is that Cordelia Gray on the basis of one novel assured herself a niche in the annals of great fictional private detectives.

Chapter Seven
The Black Tower

It was a particular place—that sinister stretch of the English coastline of Dorset "where the high cliffs of black shale tumble into the English Channel"[1]—that sparked P. D. James's imagination and gave birth to *The Black Tower* (1975), her first Adam Dalgliesh adventure in four years.[2]

Like *A Mind to Murder* and *Shroud for a Nightingale*, *The Black Tower* reflects James's twenty years experience with the British National Health Service. The novel is set at Toynton Grange, a private rest home for the disabled and terminally ill. Its owner, Wilfred Anstey, in gratitude for his miraculous cure from disseminated sclerosis at Lourdes, had devoted his property and financial resources to serving the disabled. In truth, Toynton Grange is founded on a fraud; Wilfred suffered only from hysterical paralysis. Established on deception, Toynton Grange fosters lies, deceits, and concealments among its staff and patients. This home for the physically handicapped and the incurably ill becomes a most appropriate setting for what is James's most somber book.

Dalgliesh's Recovery

The Black Tower opens with Dalgliesh, now a commander, recovering from a case of mononucleosis, so acute that the doctors had first diagnosed it as leukemia. He had reconciled himself to death. Reprieved from that verdict, he is now under a sentence of life. But because of his debilitating illness—or, perhaps as a result of a mid-life crisis—Dalgliesh feels unable to return to work. He needs time and quiet to ponder his future. A postcard from an old family friend he has not seen in years offers an ideal solution: Father Michael Baddeley, former curate to Dalgliesh's father and now a chaplain at Toynton Grange, wants to see him on an important matter. Dalgliesh decides that Dorset would be a splendid place in which to recuperate.

Toynton Grange

Toynton Grange is still another one of those structures in James that is being used for a purpose other than that for which it was designed. Unlike the elegant Georgian building that houses the Steen Clinic in *A Mind to Murder*, this Georgian home was an aberration from the time it was built, perversely facing, as it does, inland (19). But like the Steen it is now in danger of passing from the private to the public sector, and, even worse, of being converted into vacation condominiums, a sign of the times.

The inhabitants of Toynton Grange don't know whether to consider the place "a nursing home, a commune, a hotel, a monastery or a particularly dotty lunatic asylum" (89–90). It is run more as a religious society than as a hospital. Meals are eaten Trappist fashion, in silence; and Wilfred and his small staff often wear monks's robes and cowls—convenient disguises, as it turns out, for the murderer. The patients, both as therapy and as help for the home's shaky finances, make cosmetics, sold to customers as far away as Marseilles.

Arriving at Toynton Grange, Dalgliesh senses "something strange and almost sinister" (19). Two recent deaths there within a two-week period confirm his suspicions. One was that of a patient, Victor Holroyd, disliked, spiteful, soured by illness, who apparently wheeled himself over Toynton Head to the rocks below. A few days later, Father Baddeley succumbed to heart disease. There is no reason, however, to think the deaths are linked or that either was unnatural. Yet Dalgliesh is convinced that the priest's "request had sounded so clearly a sentence of death" (67).

The staff at Toynton Grange could find employment elsewhere only with difficulty. Eric Hewson, the resident medical officer, had been removed for a time from the medical register because of a sexual relationship with a sixteen-year-old patient. He and his wife Maggie, an unhappy alcoholic, live in Charity Cottage, aptly named, according to Maggie, since they live off Wilfred's largesse. Dot Moxon, the matron, had to leave her last post after striking an elderly patient. Helen Ranier, resident nurse, is carrying on a none-too-concealed affair with Hewson. Dennis Lerner, a male nurse, is a homosexual. And Albert Philby, the odd-job handy man, is an ex-con.

With Holroyd dead, only five patients are left. Young Georgie Allen is now too ill to leave his bed. Grace Willison, dull, middle-aged, and religious, puts out the home's quarterly newsletter. Jennie

Pegram writes poison pen letters to compensate for the fuss and attention she once received. Henry Carwardine resolved not to get involved in the lives of the other patients when he came to Toynton Grange; nevertheless, he fell in love with a young male polio patient. Wilfred on moral grounds had the young man removed to another hospital where he died.

Ursula Hollis finds herself in her mid-twenties a victim of venereal disease. Steve, her callous husband, disgusted and frightened by any illness, has sent her to Toynton Grange. He inquires only perfunctorily about her health and no longer even vaguely mentions relocating closer to her. He has settled down, very nicely, with his friend, Morgan Evans, who has replaced Ursula in his affections. As her disease becomes more debilitating, she becomes increasingly unhappy.

In addition to staff and patients, two others live on the home's grounds: Wilfred's widowed sister, Millicent, twice convicted of shoplifting, has a pecuniary, rather than a philanthropic, interest in Toynton Grange. Julius Court, on the other hand, has been a Good Samaritan to Toynton Grange. He is a young man of sybaritic tastes, whose face, with pouches under the eyes and a "slight-petulance" to the mouth, reveals "a trace of self-indulgence" (32).

With the exception of Wilfred and Julius, no one really wants to be at Toynton Grange, but the alternatives are even less pleasant. All are understandably bitter. All harbor guilt and resentment. All suffer, if not from physical debility, then, in Wilfred's words, "from a progressive incurable disease. We call it life" (52).

Death and Resolution

On the excuse of sorting out the books Father Baddeley has left him, Dalgliesh justifies his stay at Toynton Grange. He wants to reassure himself that the priest's call for help will not go unanswered. Ironically, his very presence at Toynton Grange and his determination to pursue the truth of the deaths there lead to subsequent murders.

Dalgliesh pokes around, asks questions, consults with the local authorities, probes into the lives of staff and patients. He knows what makes a good detective: the instinct for asking the right questions and knowing where to put the pressure. The more he investigates, the more he can smell evil. Perhaps his years as a policeman have made him reluctant to take information at face value; perhaps his illness and self-doubts as to his direction in life have sapped his intelligence as well as his strength.

Two more deaths follow: Grace Willison's death seems natural enough; she was old and terminally ill. Maggie Hewson's suicide can be attributed easily to her unhappiness. Yet if all these deaths are coincidental, then "death was becoming a little too common at Toynton" (197).

Only when the patients have set out for Lourdes and Dalgliesh is about to take off for London does an item in the local paper provide that piece to the puzzle "which, slotted into place, suddenly made sense of so many other discarded pieces" (243). Putting together all he has observed and learned, Dalgliesh comes up with the answer: drugs. The pilgrimages to Lourdes provide a convenient cover-up for illegal drug traffic. He surmises the drugs pass customs concealed in the handgrips of the wheelchairs. Through Grace's newsletter with the dates of each pilgrimage, the suppliers, distributors, and customers could be informed as to dates of consignments. The master mind behind the drug trade is Julius Court, who always saw to it that he was present when the pilgrims returned from Lourdes and who even provided a van so that the trips could continue and who is living beyond his means.

At Toynton Grange Dalgliesh is confronted by Julius and a luger. In the long confession that follows, Julius explains the motives behind and the means of the murders. The final scene takes place at the cliff's edge in view of the Black Tower, a landmark that overlooks the headlands. There is a fight to the death after Julius drops his gun, and it is Julius, not Dalgliesh, who plunges to his death.

At the novel's conclusion, Dalgliesh, recovering from a slight wound inflicted by Julius, thinks that once he leaves the hospital, he will go back to work. He was "so pleased that he wasn't going to die after all" (271).

The Black Tower as Mystery

Despite its high number of murders—more than in any other James mystery—The Black Tower is a slow moving book, "heavy-going," as the New York Times describes it.[3] As if to compensate for the snail's pace of the early chapters, the last thirty pages are overly dramatic: the killing of Philby, Dalgliesh's ride in a car trunk with the corpse, his jumping of Julius, their fight—"they fought like famished animals clawing at their prey" (268)—the last minute arrival of the police, Julius's plunge to the waters below. Much of this strains credulity.

Nothing is more incredulous, however, than Julius's confession. "Now, tell me," he asks Dalgliesh, "how you found me out. I'm assuming that you have. . . . If not, then I've miscalculated" (250). One can accuse this man who has gotten away with murder, not once but several times, of many faults, but miscalculation is not one of them. But the confession is necessary as there is no other way the reader can learn how and why the murders were committed. The confession also calls attention to the book's overly complex plot.

The Physically Handicapped

With its weak ending and its less than solid detective work, *The Black Tower* does not completely satisfy as a novel of mystery and detection. But its well-realized bleak setting—the desolate Dorset coast with its "stark embattled slabs of mutilated ashlar silhouetted high against the gentle sky" (17)—and its equally bleak atmosphere—the physical and mental stresses of the ill and dying—do impress. Indeed, the most striking aspects of the book are not the mystery and solution, but James's insights into the world of the physically handicapped and her reflections on death.

Eric Hewson, as he looks at his patients in their wheelchairs, imagines he sees broken puppets, heads slumped sideways, necks twisted. Dalgliesh at his first dinner at Toynton Grange "tried to shut his ears to the muted slobbering . . . the sudden retching" (83). "A globule of mucus" drips from Carwardine's chin as he speaks in a "high distorted voice" (83). Grace Willison finds a paperback Trollope too heavy for her to read in bed. Ursula Hollis, grimly and painfully, propels herself around her room on the top of a cushion, "her dead feet . . . white and flabby as fish on the cold floor, the toes splayed like obscene excrescences vainly scrabbling for a grip" (173). Jennie Pegram's golden hair "hung like a crimped curtain around [her] dwarfish body" (48). Dalgliesh wonders what it must be like to experience "desire, love, lust even, and be imprisoned in an unresponsive body" (135).

Uncoordinated, ugly, grotesque as the patients appear to be, Dalgliesh finds them, nonetheless, likable. Essentially a loner himself, he feels a bond with them. To suggest this link, James has Dalgliesh bring with him to Dorset a copy of Thomas Hardy's *The Return of the Native* to reread; Carwardine when his disability forced him into invalidism at Toynton planned to reread all of Hardy.

To an outsider, Ursula, Grace, Jennie, and Henry are the grotesques Hewson imagined he saw, heads nodding and wagging, limbs powerless, bodies no longer in control. But James shows us they can still respond to human emotions. They know as well as anyone else the high cost of love and hate. One might argue, as Marghanita Laski has, that the scenes dealing with Ursula's wretched marriage to the callow Steve, though "painfully well written," are "overloaded for the purposes of the crime novel."[4] But they are what make *The Black Tower* as much a serious novel of character as a novel of detection.

Death and Murder

Unnatural death, of course, is no stranger to murder mysteries. It is one of the givens, along with suspects, motives, detection, and solution. But to treat a corpse as nothing more than a piece in the puzzle is to trivialize death. Murderers play for keeps in James's books. Victims are not going to get up and take a bow, as she has said of Agatha Christie's corpses.[5] Nowhere is this truth better seen than in the exactingly described clinical picture of Maggie Hewson's body as it hangs from a banister: "The body twisted so that the flushed face slowly turned and looked down . . . with what seemed a deprecating, half melancholy, half rueful surprise at finding herself at such a disadvantage. . . . she hung elongated like a bizarre and gaudily painted doll strung up for sale. . . . One thrust of a knife and the sawdust would surely spill out from the stuffed veins to pyramid at his feet" (208–9). In death Maggie looks like her husband's vision of the patients as puppets, dangling, pulled by invisible strings at the back of their necks. This is not the polite description of a Christie victim, the body on the library floor. This is not a description of death one can simply brush off as being part of the formula for a detective novel.

But if murder is a staple for the mystery writer, death as a natural part of life is not. James, however, treats death—as opposed to murder—as legitimate a subject of inquiry as Agatha Christie's famous question, "Who killed Roger Ackroyd?" Death pervades *The Black Tower*, from the first chapter, where Dalgliesh feels despondent on learning he is not to die, through the very last chapter when he experiences profound relief "that he wasn't going to die after all" (271).

Even the chapter headings emphasize death: Death of a Priest, A Stranger in the Night, The Dreadful Shore, Act of Malice, A Bloodless Murder, Mist in the Headland, The Black Tower. Although the first chapter heading bears the word "life," it is a "Sentence of Life," thus bringing to mind the judgment of death that hangs over those living at Toynton Grange. It also suggests that though death is lonely, only life is lonelier.

That death as a living presence should be on the minds of those who live and work at Toynton Grange comes as no surprise. What needs explaining as the coroner examines Grace's emaciated body is "the mystery of continuing life [,] not the fact of death" (202).

Death is also very much on the minds of the two outsiders at Toynton Grange: Adam Dalgliesh, detective, and Julius Court, murderer. Dalgliesh's own close brush with death, the many deaths at the home, the desolate Dorset atmosphere, all bring back painful memories. When Dalgliesh was fourteen, there was a local farmer's son, shy and gentle, who, on a weekend home from his first term at college, had shot dead both of his parents, his fifteen-year-old sister, and then himself. For Dalgliesh, who had imagined himself to be in love with the girl, "it had been a horror eclipsing all subsequent horrors" (204). Erlene Hubly sees this chaotic event as "certainly one of the reasons he became a detective."[6] The pursuit of the criminal and the reestablishment of law and order became for him a protection against and a means of coping with human vulnerability and hurt. It is thus understandable that in the book in which he questions whether or not to continue in his profession, he would recall this traumatic episode.

In his mind, Dalgliesh confuses the Toynton priest officiating at Grace's funeral with Father Baddeley, who had presided over the mass funeral of the unfortunate family. Now they are all dead—the family, Father Baddeley, Holroyd, and Grace.

Are the deaths at Toynton Grange the result of murder, as Dalgliesh believes, or are they natural, as everyone insists? Can one, indeed, distinguish between natural and unnatural death? What, after all, is murder, but the inevitable hastening of the inevitable? Every death, natural or unnatural, benefits someone, lifts "a burden from someone's shoulders, whether of responsibility, the pain of vicarious suffering or the tyranny of love" (196). If one looks only at motive, as a detective does, every death is suspicious. But "every death" is "at the last . . . a natural death" (196). Dalgliesh recalls what a forensic pathologist had told him as a young detective constable years ago at his very first postmortem: "When we get them on the slab, lad, there's no such thing as unnatural death" (196).

Julius Court also thinks about life and death, but he places no high esteem on either. He is confident that what follows death is annihilation. But he feels no fear; it would be unreasonable to do so. And when one loses the fear of death, other fears become meaningless (252). Father Baddeley's faith prepared him for death. Nevertheless, Julius prepares defenses against death: money and the comforts money can buy. When these no longer suffice, then "three bullets in a Luger" are his response (109). When he confronts Dalgliesh with that luger, one bullet is for the detective, the other two for himself, should they be needed. With no fear of death, this man who trades in death—"everybody who takes hard drugs wants to die" (252)—can kill with seeming impunity.

The Black Tower

The final encounter between these two adversaries takes place in the shadow of the Black Tower. Early in his stay at Toynton Grange, Dalgliesh makes the tower the destination for a morning's walk. As he muses on Victor's death, he suddenly comes across the tower. Squat and circular, topped with an octagonal structure, faced with black shale, this Gothic edifice had been built by Wilfred's great grandfather, who walled himself in to await the Second Coming. No one knew he was there, and when he was found, dead from starvation, "he'd torn his fingers to the bone trying to claw himself out" (108), having had second thoughts about the Savior's imminent arrival. Dennis Lerner, Julius's confederate and sometime lover, sees the tower as "a symbol. . . . a folly built to amuse a child. And underneath there's horror, pain, madness and death" (109).

The "Necessi Mori" engraved on the stone plaque set in the wall of the tower's porch reminds Dalgliesh, fresh from his own brush with death, that though one could ignore death, "fear it, even welcome it," one could "never defeat it. . . . Death: the same yesterday, today and forever" (106).

Death and the Black Tower are synonymous. The tower almost becomes Wilfred's funeral pyre when Julius sets fire to it. It is Father Baddeley's presence in the tower the afternoon of Victor's death that signs his death warrant. And it is within sight of the tower that Dalgliesh and Julius fight to the death. Robin W. Winks feels the tower figures "a bit too obviously, both as symbol and reality."[7] Its effective presence, however, cannot be denied.

Science and Religion

Contributing to the novel's somber tone is James's acknowledgment that those twin bulwarks of comfort, religion and science—here, in the form of medicine—offer little consolation, and are all too often ineffective. Both Dalgliesh's and Wilfred's doctors make faulty diagnoses. Certainly Dalgliesh's close call with death robs him of his self-confidence and leaves him depressed. If, as the adage has it, a doctor's best medicine is his credibility, then these doctors are dispensing little more than nostrums. The pathologist who examines Grace's body cannot decide whether she died from a heart condition, disseminated sclerosis, or a neoplasm in the upper stomach. He never does determine the true cause of her death, a plastic bag held over her nose and mouth. There is little in this book to justify one's confidence in doctors. The bemused attitude James takes to doctors in other of her books assumes darker hues in *The Black Tower*.

If one cannot turn to medicine for assurance, neither can one turn to religion with any hope of solace. Father Baddeley's ministrations do little to relieve, let alone redeem, the gloom and wretchedness of those at Toynton Grange. Hope of eternal bliss and a loving God must be dashed anytime one passes through the main hall of the home dominated by its stained glass windows depicting a vindictive Old Testament God expelling Adam and Eve from Paradise and demanding from Abraham the sacrifice of Isaac. The patients go to Lourdes, but no one is cured; even Wilfred's miraculous cure is bogus.

Moreover, religion is often subverted for nefarious purposes. The pilgrimages to Lourdes are a convenient front for a drug operation. The Black Tower, built as a refuge to await the Second Coming, entombs Wilfred's ancestor and almost becomes his funeral pyre. It is also where Wilfred retreats not to meditate but to pore over his cache of pornography. Julius wears a monk's robe when he murders Grace. Father Baddeley is murdered as he prepares to hear confession.

Evaluation

As in James's other coastal novel, *Unnatural Causes*, Dalgliesh has no official function here. Certainly it is incumbent on him as a friend rather than as a police officer to solve the mysteries at Toynton Grange. The result is that *The Black Tower*, along with *Unnatural Causes*, is the most personal of the Dalgliesh books. This is the only Dalgliesh novel that begins not with a murder but with Dalgliesh, as he ruminates on his sudden reprieve from death. Although the novel's point of view does shift to others, Dalgliesh is the center of consciousness for most of the book.

Although most critics seem to agree with Robin W. Winks's estimate that *The Black Tower* is the least convincing of James's mysteries[8]—a distinction one might claim for *Unnatural Causes*—James has a particular fondness for the book. First, it won her a second Silver Dagger from the British Crime Writers Association. Second, the novel "marks a significant step . . . in my development as a writer."[9] Certainly *The Black Tower* does reveal a stronger emphasis on character and theme than on crime and detection. James has never felt that the crime novelist should be barred from exploring "the realities of the human condition, merely because . . . she is working within the constraints of the classical English detective story."[10] One does sense here as in *Unnatural Causes* that James is chafing somewhat under those constraints as she attempts to write a novel that is more than a mystery story. By the time of *Innocent Blood*, five years later, when James writes her first nondetective novel, those constraints will be absent.

Chapter Eight
Death of an Expert Witness

Death of an Expert Witness (1977)[1] opens with a particularly brutal murder, but it is not the one Dalgliesh is called in to solve. It does, however, serve to introduce the setting, characters, and theme of James's most powerful mystery. As in her other books, murder is again seen as a contaminating crime, violating privacy and touching everyone. As Dalgliesh investigates, he uncovers past follies, hidden fears, well-kept secrets, and personal longings.

At the conclusion of his investigation, Dalgliesh will feel an immense weariness. Perhaps there are some crimes better left unsolved, some nooks and crannies of people's lives that, for their sake and his, should go unexamined. He knows that it is not possible to do police work honestly and completely without inflicting pain (311). In the closing paragraphs of the book, the murderer will say that he has forfeited the right to feel pain. But not Dalgliesh. And not the reader, who will feel for the murderer and his victims more pain and sympathy and pity than for similar characters in other James novels.

The Setting

The setting for the story is the small town of Chevisham, not far from Cambridge, in East Anglia. A young woman, dead by manual throttling, has been found in an abandoned car in a clunch pit. The field of clunch—the local name for the soft chalk mined in the area since the Middle Ages—is an arid wasteland, strewn with litter, "dank with nettles and sour with rotting rubbish" (14). A no-man's land, it is a fit backdrop for murder. Its presence hovers over the novel in the same way that the Black Tower does in the previous Dalgliesh book; in fact, the concluding chapters of these two books are titled after those symbols: "The Black Tower" and "The Clunch Pit." The locals believe that evil emanates from the murky fen of the clunch field—a supernatural evil attributable to devil worshippers.

The circumstances of the young woman's death are routine enough: a domestic murder, a young married woman carrying on with another man. The emotions involved—jealousy, unrestrained sexual passions—are the very emotions Dalgliesh will find in his investigation of another murder; the clunch pit murder frames and parallels the murder he solves. In the closing chapter, moments before the figure of the murderer appears over the rim of the clunch pit, like some creature born from the stagnant marsh field, the clunch pit murder is solved. The girl's husband, a butcher's assistant, writes out a confession and then, with one of the knives of his trade, slits his throat. A messy business. Ironically, if it were not for the book's principal murder investigation, the police would have arrested him the day before. Murder breeds even more death. Murder is, indeed, a contaminating crime.

Hoggatt's Laboratory

For the scientists at Hoggatt's Laboratory, the examination of the evidence from the clunch pit murder is all in a day's routine. The oldest forensic laboratory in the country, established when the science of forensics was in its infancy, Hoggatt's, like other medical structures in James, started life as something else. It had been "an unsuitable Palladian mansion" (79) when in 1898 Colonel Hoggatt started his laboratory there; few of its original impressively proportioned chambers have escaped the fate of partitioning and of being furnished in a "compromise of bureaucratic orthodoxy and modern functionalism" (113). Hoggatt's former director, Dr. MacIntyre—Old Doc Mac—had tended to "let the reins slip a bit in recent years" (76); he has been replaced by Dr. Maxim Howarth, who already has "increased the work turnover by ten percent" (76), but who has not yet found the heartbeat of the place, lacking as he does the common touch of his predecessor.

The old order gives way to the new. Not only is there a new director, but Hoggatt's is slated to be torn down to make way for a new facility next door. Though new, in its half-built state, its "black bulk . . . loomed like some prehistoric monument" (264). Here, one of the most chilling scenes in James's fiction occurs, when a young girl, making her way home at night through the skeleton structure, panics when she believes a killer is tracking her.

She finds refuge in the small Christopher Wren chapel on the laboratory grounds. Now deconsecrated, it has been used as a storehouse for chemicals, a hall for concerts, a rendezvous for lovers, and a site for murder. For when Brenda Pridmore, clerical officer and receptionist at Hoggatt's, enters the chapel after her harrowing experience in the new laboratory, she finds a body, its face "dreadful in death" (268).

It is not the first corpse she discovers in the book. The night after the clunch pit murder, as Dr. Edwin Lorrimer, principal scientific officer of the biology department, works late at night in the laboratory, someone bashes in his skull with a mallet, a weapon that is evidence in another police inquiry. As a forensic laboratory, Hoggatt's is concerned only with scientific fact, not with emotions or motives, victims or suspects. But now the laboratory harbors a victim and suspects and a murderer.

Death of an Expert Witness

Because of the victim's prominence, Scotland Yard calls in Commander Adam Dalgliesh to head the investigation. He is accompanied by the personable Detective-Inspector John Massingham, "Honjohn" as he is called, since his father is a lord. Dalgliesh has been impressed by Massingham's intelligence and his capacity for work. He is also struck by "a streak of ruthlessness" in Massingham, although he knows that all good policemen must possess it (89). This streak of ruthlessness does, in fact, help solve the case.

There is no shortage of likely suspects. People felt uncomfortable with Lorrimer, feared him, or actually detested him. Howarth's half-sister, Domenica, whose relationship with Howarth is close to incestuous, had just broken off an affair with Lorrimer. Lorrimer's revenge for not getting the directorship of the laboratory has been to sleep with Dom. Even though the affair is now over, the thought of Lorrimer in Dom's bed is intolerable to Howarth. His jealousy is intense, his hatred deep. Lorrimer's cousin, Angela Foley, Howarth's secretary, had been told by Lorrimer, who deplored her lesbian marriage to the novelist Stella Mawson, that he planned to disinherit her, thus destroying her hopes that she and Stella can buy their dream cottage.

Cliff Bradley, Lorrimer's assistant, has received an adverse rating from Lorrimer; his career is now in jeopardy. The document examiner at Hoggatt's holds Lorrimer responsible for a relative's suicide. The police liaison officer harbors ill-will toward all forensic scientists; the man responsible for his daughter's death in an automobile accident had been acquitted because a forensic scientist had cracked under cross-examination. The policeman in charge of the clunch pit murder, Detective-Inspector Doyle, had been ordered by Lorrimer to keep out of the laboratory. Lorrimer suspected Doyle of stealing cannabis and substituting an inert substance.

It is only with the murder of Stella Mawson that Dalgliesh finds that "single, solid incontrovertible" clue that leads him to the killer (209). Dr. Kerrison, the medical examiner, had replaced Lorrimer in Domenica's bed. Learning of Dom's new lover, Lorrimer threatened him with the loss of his children's custody by disclosing the affair to Kerrison's unstable ex-wife. Even if Kerrison gave Dom up, Lorrimer wanted to punish him. Afraid of losing his children and realizing there was nothing more to talk about, Kerrison killed Lorrimer. Stella had to die because she possessed knowledge that could incriminate Kerrison.

Killer and Victim

James's characters, especially in their sexual fears and needs, go beyond the stereotypes that populate so many mysteries. They are credible, complex, and interesting men and women, who do not have easy answers to life's questions. They evoke from us sorrow and pity and understanding. Certainly Kerrison is one of James's most sympathetic killers.

His life is anxiety-ridden. His wife has run off with her lover, leaving Kerrison with their two children, three-year-old William and sixteen-year-old Nell. A highly strung youngster on the thin edge of losing touch with reality, Nell fears that her father loves William more than he does her.

In addition to his worries over his family, Kerrison is also concerned about his job. He is a dispirited man with the look of defeat. He smarts under his wife's accusation that he lacks the guts to be a real doctor; "messing about with the dead" is all that he's good for (9). A "connoisseur of death" is how Howarth characterizes him (14).

Reviled by Lorrimer, deserted by his wife, ensnared by Domenica, threatened by Stella, Kerrison is a hound at bay. Like so many of James's killers, he has been driven into a corner; his crime results from an inability to see any way out of his predicament save murder. If he does not rid himself of Lorrimer, he will lose his children to their neurotic mother. What else can he do but bludgeon Lorrimer? "You aren't a father," he accuses Dalgliesh as if in justification, "so you never could understand" (320). Dalgliesh, who lost his only child right after he was born, understands only too well. Pressure drives Kerrison to murder. That murder, in turn, exerts even more pressure that results in the second murder.

Although his appearances in the book are few—perhaps too few, considering he is the murderer—Kerrison is shown effectively as a loving father with a striking phrase. Summoned to the clunch pit in the early hours of the morning, he tries to get away without waking Nell and William: "Carefully, as if the gentleness of his touch could somehow silence the engine, he turned on the ignition" (6–7).

James manages to create pity for the despised Lorrimer as well. There are the small touches: the sympathetic way he handles bodies, the sign of the cross he makes over them before he begins his work, his genuine interest in Brenda's career, the loving way he tends his father. This "desiccated, pedantic, self-satisfied prude," as Stella characterizes him (35), is revealed as a man hopelessly entangled in the throes of sexual passion. Lorrimer's written but unsent love letters to Domenica expose his naked suffering, his excruciating self-pity, his "humiliating self-abasement" (169). His sexual failure with his first wife—he and Stella had been briefly married years ago—and his broken affair with Domenica make clear his uncertainties and unhappiness.

For all his arrogance and unswerving sense of rectitude, Lorrimer was as unsure of his place in life as is his killer. Both men have reached the end of their tethers: One will become the victim of a violent crime, the other its perpetrator. Victim and murderer are inextricably involved in each other's life and death. The positions could, in fact, be easily reversed. To both men, James brings a compasssion for the foibles and follies of mankind, for the human weaknesses that lead some men to murder and others to be murdered.

Unhappy Conclusion

When Dalgliesh and Massingham arrive at Kerrison's home in hope of getting the truth from Nell about her father's whereabouts the night of the murder, they find Nell ordering the housekeeper, Miss

Willard, to leave. Stung by the girl, she turns on her, telling Nell that it is William her father loves, not her, and that when he leaves the house at night, it is not for work but to make love to Domenica. Nell pleads with Dalgliesh to tell her otherwise. As Dalgliesh searches for a careful answer, Massingham, with that streak of ruthlessness Dalgliesh had noted earlier, destroys Nell's tenuous hold on reality with three simple words, "Yes, it's true" (309). It is not cases that break, Dalgliesh knows, "only the people" (315).

Nell confesses that her father had been away that night. She thought he had a showdown with Lorrimer because the biologist on an earlier occasion had ordered Nell and William from the laboratory. She thought her father had killed Lorrimer out of love for her. Like an animal in pain, she gives "a high despairing wail" that turns Dalgliesh's blood to ice (309).

At that moment, he wants never to see Massingham again, never to work with him again. What he had done was unforgiveable. Yet Dalgliesh knows that one cannot perform police work without causing someone pain.

As Kerrison goes off to jail, he is tortured by the realization of the futility of his crimes. He had murdered to keep his children and now they are lost to him forever. He feels like a dying man, for murder has put him beyond the pale of society and to be there is to be dead. When he killed Stella to prevent disclosure of the first murder, he irrevocably forfeited the right to feel pain. A man who feels no pain is a man no longer alive.

The case has been solved, but at a terrible cost: Lorrimer is dead, driven to the breaking point by sexual frustration and jealousy; Kerrison has killed to hold on to his children and has lost them; Nell's slight grasp on sanity has slipped, perhaps permanently; Bradley's career is in pieces; Doyle has been forced to resign; Angela has lost the one person she loved and who loved her. For Dalgliesh, there is more pain than satisfaction. Only Domenica is untouched, unscathed. She absolves herself of any responsibility: "It wasn't because of me" (311).

Hypocritically, she accuses Dalgliesh of being part of "a filthy trade" (310) in which "longing and loneliness, terror and despair," are neatly recorded in police reports (311). His simple reply—not unlike his answer to Mary Taylor's request of him to suppress evidence in *Shroud for a Nightingale*—is that his is a job that must be done.

Murder investigations are never agreeable. Prior to Dalgliesh's setting out for Chevisham, a colleague tells him, "Oh, you'll solve it. . . . You always do. But I'm wondering at what cost" (79). Dalgliesh does not answer. Yet he knows even then that the cost will be considerable, not only to others, but to himself as well. Nowhere else in James's fiction is one made so aware of the pain that all suffer as a result of murder.

The Pain of Loneliness

That pain is reflected in the many lonely lives, unhappy marriages, and broken relationships among the book's characters. Pain and loneliness, James is saying, are the fate of the human condition.

In a novel filled with lonely people, none is lonelier than the wan and sallow Mrs. Meakin, a widow Inspector Doyle picks up the night of the murder for a quick tumble in his car. She knows the danger of going off with strange men; she admits to being afraid as she waits by the side of the road to be picked up. "But at least I'm feeling something. It's better to be afraid than alone" (261). She is not after sex but the opportunity to talk to someone, "the consolation of a warm brightly lit bar and, always, the hope that, next time, it may be different" (261–62). When Massingham admonishes her by saying that "it's better to be alone than dead," she answers him out of her knowledge of loneliness: "You think so, sir? But then you don't know anything about it, do you" (261). Her dinner, which Dalgliesh and Massingham interrupt to question her, "three fish fingers, a mound of mashed potatoes, and peas. . . . exuding a greenish liquid in which the fish fingers were slowly congealing," sums up her drab, lonely life (257–58).

Almost as pathetic is Miss Willard, Kerrison's housekeeper, hopelessly in love with him. Her room, with its smell of "sweet sherry, unfresh body linen, and cheap scent" reflects her solitary life (231). A small wooden Madonna on a shelf only emphasizes the tawdriness of the room, yet at the same time dignifies it, "seeming to say that there was more than one kind of human loneliness, human pain, and that the same mercy embraced them all" (232).

So desperately does Lorrimer want Domenica back that he fools himself into believing that by threatening Kerrison, she will return. Lorrimer knows full well that Dom doesn't love him, but that isn't important. What he craves, like Mrs. Meakin, is another person's presence to break the monotony and fear of being alone. As for Dom, she has had many lovers, for she is easily bored, but she always returns to the company of her half-brother. "Contra mundi," against the world, has been their private code of defiance and allegiance.

Death of an Expert Witness contains four broken marriages and one that has reached the straining point. The one happy and fulfilled relationship is the lesbian one between Angela and Stella, but that is sundered by Stella's murder. Interestingly enough, the one happy relationship in *The Black Tower* is that between two homosexual men, Henry and Peter, abruptly terminated by Peter's transfer from Toynton Grange and his subsequent death.

Although homosexuality per se is never in the forefront of James's fiction—it is never, for example, a motive for murder—it "thickens the texture of the background" of several of her books.[2] We will return to this subject in the last chapter of this study. Suffice to say, James's willingness to treat of the subject is an indication of how her fiction, though operating within the formula of the classical detective story, is up-to-date in its inclusion of contemporary and controversial subject matter.

Structure and Scope

One of the longest of her novels, *Death of an Expert Witness* is also one of James's best plotted. The clues are well placed, the foreshadowing is effectively subtle, and the author is scrupulously fair. The solution is convincing; it fits the facts of the case as well as Kerrison's psychological makeup. One believes he would kill for the reasons he gives. And for the first time since *A Mind to Murder*, James does not find it necessary to arrange for her killer to die for his crime. The loss of his children and the painful knowledge of what he has done are punishment enough for Kerrison. Nor do we have the long and awkward confession scene in which the killer explains all. Dalgliesh fits the pieces of the puzzle together logically and skillfully. There are a few inconsistencies having to do with times, but none are damaging to the credibility of the solution.

The book moves along at a steady pace, the subplots crisply dovetailing into the neatly tailored main plot. James draws unobtrusive but telling parallels between the clunch pit murder and Lorrimer's. In one, the triangle is unfaithful wife, lover, and jealous husband; in the other, wanton mistress, current lover, and jealous ex-lover. In the opening scene at the clunch pit, we are introduced to the three men in Domenica's life. One will kill another; and the third, Maxim Howarth, will always be there for the woman who has destroyed the other two. In the book's closing scene, both cases will be resolved.

Though the book's tone is one with the dank, infected black fen, *Death of an Expert Witness* does contain characters who represent normality, health, stability. There is the ingenuous Brenda Pridmore. Though she discovers both corpses, she is one of the few characters untouched by what happens. Murder spoils and alters people's lives, but as Dalgliesh tells her, "You're young and intelligent and brave, so you won't let it spoil yours" (291). Brenda knows that you can't and don't hurt those who love you (290). It is this attitude as well as her knowing reference to Jane Austen's Marianne Dashwood that must endear her to Dalgliesh and must remind the reader that she displays both the sense and sensibility of Austen's heroines.

There are also some wonderfully drawn minor characters: Brenda's mother, to whom a third cup of tea and a rasher of bacon are indispensable before facing the day's problems; Mrs. Bidwell, with her perceptive, shrewd folk wisdom; and the whining old Mr. Lorrimer, who stews over missed meals and frets over broken TV sets and who might remind one of Jane Austen's Mr. Woodhouse.

Best of all, there is Winifred Swaffield, the rector's wife, one of those "excellent women" who might have stepped out of a novel by Austen or Barbara Pym. In her tweed skirt, thick brogues, openwork woolen stockings, felt hat, "its crown stabbed with a steel hatpin . . . [and] jammed uncompromisingly over a broad forehead" (154), she brings with her "a reassuring ambience of homemade jam, well-conducted Sunday schools, and massed women's choirs singing Blake's 'Jerusalem.' " If confronted by "the frayed and ragged edges of life," Mrs. Swaffield "would merely iron them out with a firm hand and neatly hem them down" (156).

James's setting for the story, a laboratory where murder investigations are a daily routine, is a brilliant stroke. But the novel is not confined to the closed community of the forensic science laboratory. Dalgliesh's first glimpse of Chevisham, spread beneath him as his helicopter prepares to land, suggests something of the scope of the book. We learn a good deal about local architecture—always an interest for Dalgliesh—including the Moonraker Inn, run by the aptly named Mrs. Gotobed (an affectionate nod to Bertha Gotobed in Dorothy L. Sayers's *Unnatural Death*). We get descriptions of a local chamber music concert and of morris dancers. The local color is not just for atmosphere; it is threaded into the fabric of the novel and provides clues and alibis.

Dominating the novel is the dreary, rank-smelling, water-logged, sullen clunch pit, a wasteland of trash and petrified trees, an appropriate symbol of the loneliness, despair, and barrenness of life that infect so many of the novel's characters.

Dalgliesh

In no other of his cases is Dalgliesh so genuinely moved and personally pained at what he encounters. Yet ironically, the reader coming upon Dalgliesh for the first time is likely to learn less about him from this book than from any others in the series. On first meeting Kerrison's children, he realizes that he really knows nothing about children. His only child had died at birth. He has convinced himself that he is lucky to have been spared coping with the traumatic years of an adolescent. Yet when talking to William and Nell—his child would now have been Nell's age—he is suddenly aware of an entire range "of human experience on which . . . he had turned his back, and that this rejection somehow diminished him as a man" (226–27). He can vicariously identify with Kerrison in his fear of losing his children.

Dalgliesh can also identify with Kerrison in his involvement with Domenica. He, too, is susceptible to her beauty and wiles. "Given the opportunity, he would . . . have done the same" as Lorrimer and Kerrison. He, too, would have become a partner in Domenica's "erotic, esoteric game" (312). The implication is that he, too, could have become victim or killer. As in *Shroud for a Nightingale*, James lets us glimpse, if only momentarily, the dark side of her detective's nature.

Dalgliesh is still the sensitive and intelligent poet; he quotes Plutarch, Orwell, and George Crabbe, whom he has always held in high regard ever since he read that Jane Austen "could have fancied being Mrs. Crabbe" (189). And in a novel where unbridled passion motivates killer and victim, that quoted line is relevant: "That one strong passion should engross it [the heart] all."

Yet Dalgliesh is even more distant here than in his other outings. Massingham finds his introspective chief at times "cold enough to be barely human" (159). Dalgliesh's arrival at Chevisham in a helicopter suggests that he is like a god from above, come down to earth to right the confusion that mortal man has wrought.

Finally, one wonders, since there has been no Dalgliesh mystery since 1977, whether he (or his creator) has found murder investigations too draining on his feelings of pain, pity, and sympathy to continue in his profession. Erlene Hubly's conclusion that Dalgliesh is often left at the end of a case "with a profound sense of disillusionment and failure" is nowhere more evident than in the closing pages of *Death of an Expert Witness*.[3]

Critical Reception

Critics have been almost unanimous in their praise for *Death of an Expert Witness*. *Newsweek*'s estimate that the novel "shines with lucidity and firm intelligence" and Robin W. Winks's conclusion that it is "well up to the standard" of her best ably sum up critical opinion.[4]

In theme the book breaks no new ground. There is the same concern with the preciousness of life and the concomitant belief that no one has the right to take it away that one finds in her other mysteries. Likewise, there is the same awareness of the contaminating effects of murder and of the passions that can envelop people and blind them. But all these topics are handled with greater confidence and skill than before.

In the satisfactions it offers as a mystery, in its evocation of place, in the depth of its characterizations, in the firmness of its writing, and in its expert examination of the anguish of loneliness, the bitterness of hate, and the destructive energies of love, *Death of an Expert Witness* represents P. D. James at her best.

Chapter Nine
Innocent Blood

Having written seven detective novels, James felt she was ready "to write a novel without using the strict conventions of the mystery form." For one thing, she wanted to work with fewer characters than were to be found in most mysteries—at least a dozen possible suspects alone in *Death of an Expert Witness*—and work with them "in depth and at greater length."[1] She wished also to expand the social, moral, and psychological bounds of her fiction. *Innocent Blood* (1980)[2] is her entry into straight as opposed to genre fiction.

But she denies that she was doing anything new in the sense of "trying to deal with human beings more realistically"; that is what she had always attempted to do.[3] Still, in the sense that *Innocent Blood* is not beholden to the traditions of the classical mystery—the closed community, murder, suspects with motive and opportunity, clues, red herrings, detective, and solution—*Innocent Blood* can be considered a breakthrough into the main stream of fiction.

It is a breakthrough also in the attention it received, far more than is usually accorded mystery novels, and in the audience it reached, readers who would not ordinarily pick up James because she writes detective stories, no matter how fine those stories might be. *Innocent Blood* was published to favorable reviews, but more than one critic expressed the wish that James bring back Adam Dalgliesh.[4] *Innocent Blood* reached a far wider audience than any of her previous books through its selection by the Book-of-the-Month Club; it also sent many readers back to her earlier books.

Plot

The impetus behind the book was twofold. A murder case some twenty years before had made an impression on James. A young man, on the way home from visiting his wife and newly born son in a nursing home, called in on his in-laws and battered them to death with a TV aerial. James remembered thinking about the newborn baby "and wondering what on earth was going to happen to him." How could one explain to a child that his father had been hanged for murdering his grandparents? How would this dreadful disclosure "affect the young person who had, as most of us do, after all, fabricated some kind of acceptable persona for himself?"[5]

The second impetus was the passage in Parliament in 1975 of the Children Act, the law that allowed adopted children who have reached the age of eighteen access to their birth records. In the novel, Philippa Rose Palfrey, adopted when she was eight, having recently turned eighteen, takes advantage of the new law to discover who her parents are. The truth is shattering. Her real father had raped a twelve-year-old girl whom her real mother had then murdered. Martin and Mary Ducton had been imprisoned for life. There he died; she, having served ten years, is about to be paroled. Philippa feels that contact with her mother will provide her with a past, that Mary can help her find out who she is.

She visits Mary in prison, and the two women decide to live together in London after Mary's release. There they will begin the painful process of getting to know each other. In Mary Philippa hopes to find someone who loves her and whom she in turn can love.

Philippa is not the only one interested in Mary Ducton. For ten years Norman Scase, the dead girl's father, has been waiting for Mary's release so that he can fulfill the vow he and his late wife, Mavis, had taken at the time of sentencing, "to find and kill the murderess" (61). A lonely, withdrawn man, Norman pursues revenge not for his daughter's sake, but for himself. If he can find the courage to commit so terrible a crime as murder, then no matter what might happen to him, "he could never again doubt his identity as a man" (69). For both Norman and Philippa, Mary holds the key to their identities.

Structure

Philippa's and Norman's stories parallel, cross, and interact with each other. Philippa had been for her adoptive father, Maurice Palfrey, a substitute for his dead son. In that she reminds Norman of his dead daughter, Julie, she becomes for him a substitute daughter. When Norman comes across Mary and Philippa smiling and laughing together in a park, he feels an aching emptiness for what might have been between himself and Julie.

Their stories come together when Philippa and Norman meet over Mary's body. James works out ingeniously the parallels and connections between the two stories. But her book's well-marked beginning, middle, and end, along with a brief epilogue that tells what happened to the major characters, seems more appropriate to the mystery novel than to a nongenre novel.

Despite the presence of interlocking stories, there are times when two separate novels bid for attention in the same book. One is serious and has as its core Philippa's relationship with her natural mother and her adopted father. The other, subordinate to Philippa's, is a harrowing melodramatic novel of suspense to which James brings all her considerable talents as a mystery writer. James does not always bring this fusion of the serious and the suspenseful off. Furthermore, Norman's search for his daughter's killer is more compelling than Philippa's for love and self.

With its twists and turns of plot, its revelations and climaxes, its center of attention a murder that took place in the past and one that is about to take place, and its cover-up of an attempted murder, *Innocent Blood* does not entirely abandon the world of the mystery novel. There is even a private detective whom Norman hires in his search for Mary. Both Philippa and Norman are, in a way, amateur detectives, she searching for the truth about her past, he hunting down the killer of his daughter. In a humorous aside, Philippa thinks Norman would have made a good writer of thrillers with his methodicalness, his "obsessive, guilt-ridden" preoccupation "with trivia" (294). There is even, says James, a clue in the early pages of the book as to Philippa's past and her relationship with her mother that should lead "readers to think something has gone very wrong," but "nobody ever picks it up."[6] Indeed, so pervasive are the ingredients of the thriller that more than one critic has noted that James could not entirely transcend the genre in which she had first made a name and that her breakthrough was by no means complete.[7]

Parental and Marital Relationships

Nevertheless, *Innocent Blood* is more than a thriller. In a murder mystery, the central question is the identity of the killer: "Whodunit?" In *Innocent Blood*, the central question is the identity of the self: "Who am I?" In attempting to answer this question, Philippa undertakes one of the great archetypal searches in literature, that for a father, though here James gives it a twist by substituting mother for father. Not for the first time, either, in James. Mark Callender in *An Unsuitable Job for a Woman* seeks the truth of his parentage, the identity of his mother.

Like all relationships, that between Mary and Philippa develops its own identity as it grows; eventually it becomes the means by which each woman can come to terms with her past and with herself. At times the relationship offers comfort and security. At other times it drains individual resources. But always it changes and develops, especially as a new truth about the initial basis of the relationship comes to light. Throughout the book, James balances and measures the bonds of love and obligation imposed by blood ties against those imposed by environmental ties. In this respect it is interesting to note that at one time James thought of calling the book, *The Blood Tie*.

The most important environmental tie is Philippa's relationship with her adoptive father, Maurice Palfrey, a sociologist turned TV personality. Philippa believes Maurice adopted her "for the glory of sociological theory" (35). Believing that environment and not heredity determines and develops personality, Maurice, when he first saw Philippa, felt something could be made of her (279). Pygmalion to her Galatea, Maurice has succeeded. Philippa, who remembers nothing about her life prior to the adoption, has "inherited" many of Maurice's tastes and opinions as well as his seemingly uncaring outlook on life.

Convinced that he does not love her, Philippa has fostered fantasies that she is an illegitimate child, the offspring of a romance between a serving maid and a lord. At the same time that she rebels against Maurice, she is also drawn to him. Her attitude toward this attractive male and surrogate father is not unlike Cordelia's feelings toward Dalgliesh in the last chapter of *An Unsuitable Job for a Woman*.

In a showdown with Philippa, Maurice forces her to stop "living in a fantasy world" and to face reality (271). She has substituted for the fantasy of an aristocratic father another, the fantasy that Mary had given her up for adoption because of the murder. The reality is that Mary did not want her child; not "cut out for motherhood" (273), she had given Philippa up before the rape and murder.

Mary Ducton never desired Julia Scase's death the way Philippa now wills Mary's death: "I wish they'd hanged you nine years ago," she tells Mary. "I wish you were dead" (284). Running from the flat, she wanders the streets of London. Slowly she begins to see that she and Mary are inextricably bound by a tie "stronger than hate or disappointment or the pain of rejection" (289). As André Maurois notes, "Without a family, man, alone in the world, trembles with the cold." She returns to the flat with her new recognition, but Mary is dead, the victim of an overdose of sleeping pills. Philippa had gotten to her with her words of hate before Norman could get to her with his knife. Mary's suicide is another example of James seeing to it that a murderer pays for her crime with her life.

In the epilogue we learn that Philippa and Maurice have been to bed together, "an affirmation, a curiosity satisfied, a test successfully passed" (310). Now they can resume "their roles of father and daughter" (310). The implication is that Philippa can now have a normal sexual relationship with a man, her only other previous experience having been an unsuccessful coupling with a bisexual male. James's use of incest in *Innocent Blood* to resolve the Philippa-Maurice relationship recalls the Domenica-Howarth relationship in *Death of an Expert Witness* and anticipates Clarissa Lisle's advances to her stepson in *The Skull beneath the Skin*.

Like Maurice, Norman Scase sees Philippa as surrogate child—Julie was only a few years older than Philippa—and as a sexually attractive woman. Her care and concern for him, after he has plunged his knife into the already dead body of Mary, are "more erotic—and more tender—than any other we see from her."[8] She hopes that Norman will eventually "find his patch of rose garden" (311). He does, but it will not contain a rose—Philippa's given name is Rose—but a violet: Violet Tetley, a young blind girl he has befriended. She is Philippa's alter-ego: quiet, shy, loving, caring. An orphan, Violet lost her eyesight at eight, the age Philippa was when she was adopted. Violet is literally blind to the world around her, Philippa, figuratively to the truth.

Innocent Blood is also James's fullest treatment of marital relationships, especially the painful side of marriage. Norman and Mavis Scase's marriage is haunted and doomed by Julie's murder. They feel they have failed one another. Mary Ducton has deprived them of the love they once had and has left them with nothing but hate. The one desire that now possessed them was the desire for revenge. Mary and Martin Ducton had married not out of regard or affection or love or lust, but rather out of need: his to find a woman strong enough to lead him from the temptation of young girls; hers, to find someone totally unlike her father who beat her as a child. When Martin wants

them to enter a suicide pact after the rape and murder, she refuses—
a failure in love, as she later acknowledges. Both of Maurice Palfrey's
marriages are based on deception—the first on his belief that Helen,
his first wife, was carrying his child; the second on his assumption
that Hilda, his second wife, could be taught to meet his complex
needs. But if Hilda fails him in this regard, he also fails her: she
wants children and he has kept from her the fact that he cannot father
any.

James's treatment of the strains of parental and marital relationships is compelling. But it is not directed to any clear conclusion,
nor sufficiently linked to her other concerns—good and evil, guilt and
remorse, grace and forgiveness, justice and revenge—so as to give *Innocent Blood* an overriding unity or sense of purpose.

In classical mystery stories, the puzzle provides that unity. James,
to be sure, underplays the importance of the puzzle in her mysteries.
She gives as much attention, if not more, to a detective troubled by
uncertainties, anxieties, and shortcomings we can recognize and identify with; to characters whose actions are motivated by their personalities rather than by plot exigencies; and to moral and psychological
concerns that enlarge the dimensions of her mysteries. Yet even in
those mysteries that in their richness of theme and complexity of
character come closest to straight fiction—*Shroud for a Nightingale* and
Death of an Expert Witness—there is still a puzzle to be solved, a killer
to be unmasked. The puzzle provides the center of reference, the focal
point for which themes and psychological insights are the spokes of
the wheel. But there is no puzzle in *Innocent Blood*. For puzzle James
has substituted characterization. And, as Julian Symons succinctly
puts it, "Judged by its characters, *Innocent Blood* is strikingly implau-
sible."[9]

Characterization

The problem one has with the characters in *Innocent Blood* is their
believability. James is partly successful with Norman Scase, one of
life's little men, plagued by bad luck from birth. Ugly in face and
borne down in spirit, he has led a life of quiet desperation. He is
awash with guilt over Julie's death. We are convinced that he could
track Mary Ducton down, for he brings to his task of stalking her the
same efficiency, methodicalness, and concern for detail he has brought
to his years as a middle level government clerk.

One is less convinced, however, that Norman has as sure an understanding of human psychology as James endows him with. Moreover, could such a pathetic little man have the nerve for murder? We are told that as a child Norman was called by an aunt a "proper little Crippen," a reference to the infamous Edwardian wife killer who, like Norman, was mild-mannered and sweet-tempered (111). Still, it is difficult to see him plunging his knife into Mary's throat unhurriedly, in "a ritual of justice and expiation" (211).

The challenge James faced with Mary Ducton was how to temper the heinousness of her crime so as to win reader sympathy and make it easier for Philippa to accept and love her mother. One way is to distance Mary from the crime. When she writes out her account of the events for Philippa, it is in the third person and written with a good deal of elegance that robs the crime of its horror. In it she describes truth as a butterfly that one might pin down to display its colors, "but then it wasn't a butterfly anymore" (155). But the truth is not as elusive as Mary would make it out to be.

There are also, we are to understand, extenuating circumstances. Mary had been a battered child; as an adult she could not stand to hear a child cry. In a way the weeping Julie Scase had been strangled by the child Mary had been (165). Philippa, as a baby, could not stop crying—one reason Mary put her up for adoption. So we are made to moderate our sympathies for the tear-stained Julie Scase, an unattractive child, and transfer them to the psychological victim of the tragedy, Mary Ducton.

Moreover, Mary describes Martin Ducton, the rapist, as a "gentle, timid, weak" man who hadn't hurt Julie (81). Mary tells Philippa: "It was a technical rape, but he wasn't violent. . . . you musn't picture it as worse than it was" (81). This, of course, begs the question: Rape is always a violent crime. There can be no ameliorization. Philippa, however, seems satisfied with her mother's explanation.

In many ways Mary is unbelievable as a character. We are asked to believe that her ten years in prison have had only positive effects on this psychologically scarred woman. We are asked to believe that during her imprisonment she read Shakespeare and the Victorian novelists and that she emerged from prison a highly educated woman, one who can hold her own in a discussion of George Eliot's *Middlemarch*. In the weeks following her release, she and Philippa take a culture tour of London, viewing the Mazzuoli Marbles at Brompton Oratory and an exhibit of Victorian paintings at the Royal Academy. No wonder a reviewer remarked that Mary "sounds as if she's about to take her orals in English literature."[10]

On the whole, James's characters are a disagreeable lot. "Uniformly distasteful," is how Norma Siebenheller describes them, "cruel, selfish, mean, and unhappy." They are emotional misfits "bent on the destructive aspects of human relationships."[11] Philippa Palfrey is a case in point. She is a cold, ungiving, unpleasant young woman, but then James wanted her to be regarded that way—neither likable nor lovable.[12] Because Philippa believes she was adopted for her intelligence, she has fine tuned it to the exclusion of affection, kindness, concern for others, compassion. As she is the first to admit, she is "not particularly lovable" (9).

When Jane Austen wrote *Emma* (1816), P. D. James's favorite novel, she created a heroine she was sure no one but herself would like very much. Emma's errors of judgment do cause unhappiness and injury to others; but what keeps her from completely losing our respect—for we do like her despite what her creator said—is Austen's ironic view of her. In *Innocent Blood*, however, we are asked to view Philippa not ironically, but seriously. Yet so many of her actions are improbable that we begin to doubt that outstanding characteristic of hers—her intelligence.

For one thing, it is hard to believe that an eighteen-year-old with no memory of her mother and with no knowledge of her save that she murdered a child would set up housekeeping with her without a moment's hesitation. It is also hard to accept that she would react with such sangfroid when she discovers Mary dead and a stranger sitting beside the body with a blood-stained knife. To be sure, Cordelia Gray reacts to Bernie Pryde's suicide with the same composure Philippa evinces. Further, in both *An Unsuitable Job for a Woman* and *The Skull beneath the Skin*, she faces dangerous and murderous men without any hesitation. Yet we never call her behavior into question as we do Philippa's. We expect private eyes, even one as vulnerable as Cordelia, to confront corpses and killers without flinching. As Bruce Harkness explains, we accept Cordelia's behavior "because we are within the tradition of mystery fiction." We find Philippa's "unsatisfactory precisely because we are in the straight novel."[13] Finally, it strains credulity that Philippa, whose only prior sexual experience had been a fiasco, would go to bed with her adoptive father and then consider their night together "no longer important" (310).

Equally defeating in our accepting Philippa as a believable charac-

ter, let alone a sympathetic one, is the fact that her responses to life
are, more often than not, in terms of literature. She has an apt literary quotation for every situation—a regular walking Bartlett's. She
can recall a reference to a minor English novelist, L. P. Hartley,
quote Heine's last words in French, and recite lines from Donne and
Blake, whose words "fell into her mind" (254).

The most improbable examples occur at moments of great crisis.
Learning that her father had raped a child whom her mother then
murdered, "some words of Bunyan"—a writer she does not particularly like—"came into her mind and she found herself speaking them
aloud" (21). When she discovers her mother's dead body, Dylan
Thomas's "Do Not Go Gentle into That Good Night" comes to
mind, along with images of corpses at Belsen, of bloated bodies of
children dead from starvation in Ethiopia, and of dead soldiers lying
on battlefields (291–92).

It's possible, of course, that a character like Philippa might well
think in literary tags and lines; her penchant for doing so, however,
robs her of warmth and makes her less than sympathetic. One suspects that she, as well as other characters, quote lines from literature
as much as they do because James thought this would make the novel
more literary. Even the private detective that Norman hires quotes a
line from Thomas Mann! After a while the characters sound alike and
the novel sags under a heavy weight of literary seriousness.

James's mysteries have always contained their share of literary cita-
tions and allusions, and these details do give the books a literary
flavor. But then, British detective fiction is often embellished with
literary allusions. What is a convention in that genre, however, is not
in straight fiction. In *Innocent Blood*, the quotations are artificial and
forced.

Images and Symbols

Quotations and allusions are not the only means James uses to suggest the literary and serious nature of her novel. She also uses imagery
and symbolism to a greater extent than in her mysteries. Floral images, especially roses, dominate the book. Rose is Philippa's given
name; she often wonders why Mary does not use it. Roses are found
everywhere. One of Philippa's fantasies is of her mother, a slim,
golden-haired figure standing in a rose garden. She sees a single rose
petal "like a drop of blood" (20) when she looks down at the pave-

ment after hearing the truth about her parents. There are rosebuds on the curtains in the hospital room of Norman's dying wife, Mavis; and on the cold November day that Mavis dies, Norman, sitting in St. James's park, notices a few rose buds "blighted by the cold, their stems choked with dead leaves" (62).

There is a mixed bunch of roses in the social worker's office; the wallpaper of the flat is patterned in rosebuds; roses grow in the garden where Maurice first sees and meets Philippa; and roses swing gently over her head when Norman suddenly encounters Philippa and Mary in a park. Mary is smelling an orange rose at the time, and when Norman later recalls the meeting, he remembers the rose-drenched air.

Maurice's disclosure to Hilda that he cannot father children is provoked by Hilda's clumsy attempt to arrange roses in a bowl. The roses remind him of Philippa, who usually did the flower arranging. He becomes annoyed that she has gone, leaving him with only Hilda. He decides "that he didn't like roses." They "confuse the senses," and he wonders why he ever imagined they gave him pleasure. He thinks that flowers should be judged not by how they look in vases, but "by how they grew." By this measure, rose gardens "always looked messy." The roses look beautiful for a brief moment or two before the petals bleach and peel, "littering the soil" (216).

During this conversation, Hilda pricks her thumb on a rose, leading her to quote a line from Tennyson. She tells Maurice she is going to get a stray dog that "no one has claimed" to love and care for. She will keep it away from Maurice's flower beds: "I know how you feel about the roses" (220). The scene ends with a reference to Jane Austen. Although they are seemingly talking about roses and dogs, the real but unspoken topic is, of course, Philippa and their feelings toward her.

Water, as a symbol of cleansing and purification, has an important symbolic role in the story. After mother and daughter move into the flat, Philippa throws Mary's suitcase containing all that she brought from prison into the Grand Canal. As she does so, she feels a sense of relief as if she had cast away "something of herself, of her past" (153). Mary can now put down the onus of the past and assume "the burden of happiness" (151). "That's done," she says to Philippa. "Let's go home" (153).

In a parallel scene, after the stormy confrontation with her mother, Philippa throws the sweater Mary had knitted for her into the swollen

waters of a canal. Its sleeves, "stretched out," looked like "a drowning child," the child Philippa had been. As the sweater sinks, she
feels "a physical sense of release" (286–87). Having broken her ties
with the past in the first episode, she breaks the new ties she has since
formed with her mother. She is then chased by a street gang—the
outward manifestation of her fears—and escapes. Now, "completely
alone" (289), she realizes the nature of love; she is ready to go back
to her mother with a new understanding. The first episode concludes
with Mary's words, "Let's go home." The second episode ends with
Philippa's decision to return to Mary and say, "I have come home"
(290).

If not original, the ritual acts of cleansing and the roses are effective as symbols. The trouble is that at times James moves them to
the forefront and deliberately underscores their meaning as if to an-
nounce what she is doing. At such times we become all too aware of
a conscious literary quality she is striving for. The literary seriousness
is often at the expense of the human equation.

Atmosphere

Innocent Blood is notable for its strong visual sense of place and atmosphere and for the richness of detail by which scenes come alive.
One feels, tastes, and smells contemporary London, its parks, its
shops, its offices, its neighborhoods, its seedy houses, its transporta-
tion system.

There are a number of fine set pieces of descriptive writing: the
prison at Melcombe Grange; the bleak landscape of the Midlands; Re-
gent Park; the empty streets of North Kensington through which
Philippa runs; and Delaney and Mell streets on a Saturday market
day, thronging with life, rich with vitality. Happily these scenes are
never overburdened with an excess of detail. Much of the description
comes through Philippa's eyes. Maurice has taught her to look carefully and searchingly at buildings, just as Bernie Pryde had taught
Cordelia Gray. Norman's sharp eye serves him well in the descriptions we see from his vantage point.

The moral world of the novel may strike us as dim, nightmarish,
"a murky . . . universe of crime," in Clifton Fadiman's words,[14] but
its shops, museums, and buildings are recognizable. By contrast, unfortunately, the characters pale against the backdrop of these convincingly drawn settings.

As a balance to the novel's serious tone and somber atmosphere, there are passages that reveal James's sharp wit and her amused attitude toward people and their behavior. The chairs in a social worker's office are "easy chairs" in which "no visitor had ever sat at ease" (4). Hilda in her kitchen is compared to "a high-priestess . . . among the impedimenta of her craft" (29) Maurice is bemused by his first wife's "moral eccentricity" by which she could "without compunction, father on him another man's child, yet . . . [be] outraged by the thought of abortion" (23). At Sid's Plaice, a fish-and-chip restaurant, where one "needed strong nerves although not necessarily a strong stomach" to eat (172), there is a dishwasher with "a sixteenth-century galleon in full sail" tattooed on her forearm. A waitress watches with fascination as the dishwasher plunges "her arms in the detergent foam and let[s] the bubbles froth" around the ship. " 'Make it sink,' " she cries, " 'Make it sink' " (173). There is an amusing picture of a bishop Maurice bests on a TV talk show. He wears on his face "the embarrassed, slightly ashamed and conciliatory half-smile of a man who knows that he is letting down the side, but hopes that no one but himself will have noticed it" (184–85).

Evaluation

Writing in the *Christian Science Monitor*, Barbara Phillips puts her finger on the basic flaw of *Innocent Blood* when she says that Philippa "sounds programmed."[15] This is true of the book as a whole. Everything has been so carefully calculated and contrived, with no missteps or false starts possible, that the characters have no room in which to breathe, no chance to develop on their own, no opportunity to get off the treadmill James has put them on. The human situation does not, like a puzzling murder mystery, "yield easily to solution."[16] Life does not always end "happily ever after" as it does here—and as it does not in James's own mysteries, such as *Death of an Expert Witness*. One comes away from *Innocent Blood* impressed by the skillful plotting, the strong writing, and the strikingly evoked settings; but one also feels that although "good novelists rarely write bad novels . . . some of the strongest writers have a very narrow range."[17]

Chapter Ten
The Skull beneath the Skin

With *The Skull beneath the Skin* (1982)[1] P. D. James returned to the straightforward detective story. She was aware that she might be inviting criticism from those readers who liked *Innocent Blood* and hoped to see her continue in that vein, but she wanted "to go back to the traditional detective story with a closed circle of suspects."[2] More than any of her other mysteries, *The Skull beneath the Skin* employs many of the conventions and traditions of the classical English mystery story. For James the fascination in writing the book was "in bringing these well-worn conventions up to date and in confronting them with the courage, the dispassionate intelligence, and the cool common sense of my young contemporary, female detective."[3] For the book heralds the return, after a nine-year absence, of Cordelia Gray, the appealing heroine of *An Unsuitable Job for a Woman*. In the intervening years Pryde's Detective Agency, of which Cordelia is sole proprietor, has gotten a name for itself in finding lost dogs and cats, following unfaithful husbands, and tracking down runaway teenagers. It is with hope and excitement, then, that Cordelia accepts what promises to be "a real job" (22).

The Poison Pen Letters

Sir George Ralston, a martinet with conservative leanings, hires Cordelia as bodyguard, nursemaid, and investigator for his wife, Clarissa Lisle. A fading actress, Clarissa has been receiving death threats decorated with the skull and crossbones and written in words from the plays of Shakespeare, Marlowe, and Webster that she has performed. High strung as she is, these missives of death threaten to bring to an end both her career and her sanity.

Clarissa is a thoroughly unpleasant woman, even more so than is usual for actresses in detective fiction. Though she may be losing her hold on the stage, she has not lost the capacity to inflict wounds with her cruel barbs, alienating those closest to her. Even when not on stage, she is playing a role; her rare acts of kindness are played to a full house and cost her little.

Terrified as she is of dying, Clarissa has gathered around her those who have the most to gain by her death. They are to be the audience for her latest theatrical venture, an amateur production of John Webster's *The Duchess of Malfi*. Perhaps by playing Webster's doomed duchess, she might herself somehow avoid the real thing. By living in the make-believe world of the play, she can defy death. The duchess may be murdered, but Clarissa, the actress, will take the final bow.

Courcy Island

The play is to be performed in a small, splendid Victorian theater that Ambrose Gorringe, an effete, elegant, and eccentric millionaire has restored on Courcy Island, a few miles off the Dorset coast. There Ambrose has established his domain in a medieval castle of rose-red brick.

There also is housed his collection of necrophiliac Victoriana: broadsheets advertising hangings, Staffordshire figures of murderers, part of a hangman's rope, blood-stained clothing, and his latest acquisition, a marble baby's arm, replica of a limb of one of Queen Victoria's children. The arm reminds its seller of death (27), arouses "fear and repulsion" in Clarissa, and strikes Cordelia as "unpleasant . . . and morbid" (74).

In addition to this chamber of horrors, Courcy Castle has a crypt. One of its walls is covered with grinning skulls, many of which could tell ghoulish stories; Courcy Island is accustomed to murder. During World War II, Nazi sympathizers were interned there. Suspecting that one of their own was a spy or informer, the internees bound him in an underground cavern, the Devil's Kettle, where, chained to an iron ladder, he "died slowly in the darkness" (132). To visit the Devil's Kettle is to descend "into the hell of the past" (136). It assuredly sets "the mood for the horrors" of the Webster play (121).

But horror is not to be confined to the stage—nor to crypts and caverns. Clarissa is upstaged by death, the real protagonist of this novel. A few hours before the performance, she is bludgeoned to death in her bed. Her face is a pulpy "sticky mess," the blood "darkening and clotting and oozing serum" (144). On a nearby tea tray rests the marble limb with its "chubby blood-stained fingers" (144).

This corpse will not arise to thundering applause at the end of the play. Death has taken the last bow.

Cast of Characters

Although the play's cast and audience are to come by launch from Speymouth, a harbor town of terraced Georgian houses, Ambrose has as weekend guests some close friends and relatives of Clarissa. Most have motives for wanting her dead, arising from tangled relationships, professional and amorous, present and past.

Simon Lessing, Clarissa's seventeen-year-old stepson, had seen her destroy his parents' marriage by running off with his father, since drowned; and he holds her responsible for driving his mother to an early death from grief. Recently, Clarissa had become his benefactress, either because of a sense of obligation or, more likely, because her recent marriage to the wealthy Sir George affords her the opportunity to act generously. An obsessively self-concerned youth, Simon feels he has disappointed her and that she might stop financial aid.

Sir George loves his wife, even though it is common knowledge, even to him, that she has been unfaithful. Although he had told Cordelia that business would keep him away from Courcy, he shows up a few hours before the murder. Roma Lisle, Clarissa's cousin and only blood relative, has come to Courcy to borrow money from Clarissa to keep her left-wing bookshop solvent and thus secure the wavering affections of her married lover and partner. A bristly, embittered woman, Roma has been turned down in her request. But if Clarissa dies childless, Roma stands to inherit a sizable fortune.

Tolly, Miss Tolgarth, Clarissa's dresser, has a very good motive. Clarissa had failed to give Tolly a message about her seriously injured child in fear of losing her services at a very critical moment (and quick costume change) in a production of *Macbeth*. After the performance, the hospital called to say the child was dead. Since then, this dour woman has smouldered with repressed resentment, though on the surface she is a model of the loyal servant.

It turns out that Ivo Whittingham, theater critic and Clarissa's old friend and former lover, is the father of that dead child. He would have nothing to lose by killing Clarissa as he is now divorced from his wife, alienated from his children, and dying from cancer.

As for Ambrose Gorringe, the perfect host, solicitous of his guests' needs, he could, according to Ivo, have "fun" with his theater, once he's gotten rid of Clarissa, "a particularly persistent invader" of his private domain (90). Yet if this is the way he feels about her, why has he asked her to perform in his theater?

Finally, there are the servants: Munter, the butler, a sinister-looking man with a lugubrious face; his stolid, taciturn wife; and Oldfield, the boatman and general factotum.

Final Curtain

Awaiting the police, Cordelia notes that Clarissa's silver jewel case is missing. In a secret drawer she kept a review of a performance she gave in Speymouth in 1977, "the most important notice I ever had," she informs Cordelia (112). Why this should be and why the clipping is larger than the space taken by the review bothers Cordelia. Perhaps the clipping, absurd as it might seem, has something to do with the murder.

When she finally gets to Speymouth and digs up a copy of the clipping, she finds on its reverse side a photograph of a Speymouth crowd awaiting the arrival of the Queen. "To the right of the photograph was the slightly blurred figure" of Ambrose Gorringe (291)—and this at a time when he was supposed to be out of the United Kingdom for tax purposes. If he returned for any reason, even if for an hour, he would be liable for all the tax he had avoided paying on large royalties from a very successful book. The tax would probably have been more than he spent on restoring the island and castle; moreover, he could be prosecuted for fraud.

It is obvious what had happened. Clarissa had seen the photo, realized its implications, and blackmailed Ambrose. He had been forced to abandon his privacy and turn over his domain to her. "Clarissa made use of the castle as if she were its chatelaine" (292).

When Cordelia confronts Ambrose, he admits to writing the death threats. But he had not killed Clarissa. She was already dead when he came to her bedroom.

Clarissa liked to make love before a performance, and who was available, who was new, but Simon? At his expressions of disgust, she taunted him with his sexual failure; he was no more effective than his father. Simon then struck her with the jewel case. It was Ambrose who covered up the crime; he could not risk the police finding the clipping.

Cordelia finds Simon in the Devil's Kettle, where he has handcuffed himself to the stairs, dropped the key, and awaits death by water. Ambrose had told him that the police were on his trail and that he would be incarcerated for life, a future he could not face.

Diving for the key, she finds it and releases him. But Ambrose has shot the bolts of the trapdoor, leaving them to drown. She leads Simon through the cavern's narrow aperture to the sea. Cordelia "was swimming for her life. . . . The sea was death, and she struggled against it" (317). She is picked up by the fisherman who only a short time before had returned her to Courcy from Speymouth. Despite his being a good swimmer, Simon does not make it: "Weakened by cold and terror and perhaps by some despair which went beyond them, he hadn't been strong enough" (319). Like his father before him, he drowns.

It is now Cordelia's word against Ambrose's. Simon is dead, and Ambrose has burned the clipping. She knows he is a fighter who won't "yield an inch now or later" (326). Still, she will not back down. She will unhesitatingly tell the truth and survive. "Nothing could touch her" (328).

"The Skull beneath the Skin"

James's title comes from T. S. Eliot's "Whispers of Immortality" (1920) and refers to the Jacobean playwright John Webster: "Webster was much possessed by death / and saw the skull beneath the skin." Stephen Spender writing of Eliot, says that he enters "into that sensuality of the post-Elizabethan era which identifies passionate feelings about love with those about death—flesh and skeleton."[4]

The atmosphere of Webster's plays permeates the novel. His are plays of vengeance with monstrous deeds that arise from the characters's emotions and passions. Ivo describes Webster as a "charnel-house poet" whose *The Duchess of Malfi* is "a highly stylized drama of manners, the characters mere ritual personifications of lust, decadence, and sexual rapacity, moving in a pavane toward the inevitable orgiastic triumph of madness and death" (81). In a slightly exaggerated way this describes the action of the novel: a weekend in the country—in this case, on an island—with civilized men and women that ends in murder engendered by sexual appetite and greed.

The fascination with evil and death that is Webster's hallmark can be found in James's novel in the Grand Guignol trappings of the

mystery: death masks, grinning skulls, a claustrophobic crypt, the
ghostly apparitions Cordelia sees at night, the Devil's Kettle, a tor-
ture chamber of death—"a deep pit of darkness," to use words from
Webster's *The Duchess of Malfi*.

As in Webster, the outward horrors evoke the gloomy moral world
the characters inhabit, the macabre and menacing aspects of the human heart and soul. James's stage props of horror do not frighten as
much as do the wickedness and evil that humans are capable of. Joseph Conrad in *Under Western Eyes* (1911) writes, "The belief in a supernatural source of evil is not necessary; men alone are quite capable
of every wickedness." A man can be as evil as his wants demand. We
shiver at delight at the skulls and bones, but we cringe with terror
at the dark and all too real compulsions of men and women.

Cordelia Gray

Clarissa may portray the Duchess of Malfi on stage, but it is Cordelia who shines like Webster's heroine with courage and dignity. She
is, as Ivo observes, "possessed of that divine common sense which is
impervious to the blandishments of egotism" (89). She reaches out to
human beings in distress, for if she does not, she thinks, "if you
opted out long enough from human concerns, from human life with
all its messiness, you opted out also from human pity" (326).

Young as she is—and she often seems here younger than her
years—and vulnerable as she appears, with her gentle face, delicate
hands, and modest mien, Cordelia is resolute. Staring evil in the face
at the novel's conclusion, she will not waver from her steadfast purpose.

One cannot help but feel, however, that James has too consciously
made Cordelia a shining beacon in a dangerous world, trying to save
lives from being wrecked on the rocks. Cordelia has become a bit too
serious, a bit too proper, and a bit less interesting than in *An Unsuitable Job for a Woman*. She wishes, for instance, that detecting did not
require "such a weight of deception" (85), a surprising thought from
one who tried to cover up a murder in her earlier case. Moreover, she
is burdened by a sense of failure, blaming herself for Clarissa's death
and thinking it presumptuous of her to accept money from Sir George
"for so tragic a failure" (297). She broods too much over her effectiveness as a detective, so much so that Michele Slung finds her "a sad

sack" with a "vulnerability . . . close to self-pity." Further, Slung sees her suffering from a St. Joan complex: Cordelia is "noble and courageous and listening to the wrong voices."[5]

Parody and Self-Parody

Situated only a few miles off the coast of Dorset, Courcy Island will remind the reader of Agatha Christie's Indian Island, a few miles off the coast of Devon in *Ten Little Indians* (1939). Indeed, *The Skull beneath the Skin* conjures up a host of English country house mysteries.

In the tradition of these books, all the familiar ingredients are here: a none-too-accessible setting, a closed circle of suspects—including such stock types as the temperamental actress, the conservative peer, the disgruntled poor relative, a sardonic theater critic, the devoted companion, the sensitive, lonely youth, the efficient butler—and hovering in the wings, the unknown intelligence directing the action, manipulating the characters.

James uses the conventions with deliberate parody. Ambrose sardonically points out that Clarissa's murder "is a storybook killing" (166). As Inspector Grogan runs down his "choice bunch of suspects" (184), he is reminded there is even a butler, whose presence he regards "as a gratuitous insult on the part of fate" (185). After the butler accidentally dies, Ambrose observes that a dead suspect is very convenient: He cannot deny what others say about him; he cannot prove that he did not commit the crime. But, he adds, nobody would believe that "the butler did it." "Even in fiction . . . that solution is regarded as unsatisfactory" (260).

Cordelia feels a "claustrophobic unease" when she realizes that the only lifelines to the mainland, the telephone and the launch, could be "both easily put out of commission" (96). It occurs to her with "stark and frightening logic" that there are ten people on this isolated island and that one of them is a killer (244). Sergeant Buckley is of the opinion that with one of these ten a murderer, all but one will probably "sleep behind locked doors" (230). Time and again we are reminded of stock-in-trade elements from countless mystery novels of the past.

In some way or another, as Hanna Charney has written, "detective novels are often filled with allusions to books"—to an entire work or its title or its theme or quotations from it. So widespread is this use of a book-within-the-book that at times this principle "becomes the basis for the construction of the work."[6]

Examples abound of mystery writers using books or plays—for theater can serve the same function as a book—as titles or themes or sources of quotations or structural devices. Agatha Christie's *The Labor of Hercules* (1947) is built around the myth of Hercules's labors; the nursery rhyme "Who Killed Cock Robin" becomes the structural center of S. S. Van Dine's *The Bishop Murder Case* (1929). The chapters to Dorothy L. Sayers's *Gaudy Night* (1935) are headed by quotations from Renaissance writers. *Macbeth* figures prominently in Ngaio Marsh's *Light Thickens* (1982) as does *Hamlet* in Michael Innes's *Hamlet, Revenge* (1937), whose basic situation—a murder during a private performance of the play—is not unlike that in *The Skull beneath the Skin*. The titles to Ruth Rendell's mysteries come from Beaumont and Fletcher, Michael Drayton, Wordsworth, Poe, and Shakespeare. Shakespeare also provides Simon Brett with the title of his *So Much Blood* (1977) while Thomas Hood furnishes the chapter headings. Swinburne is the source of the title of Patricia Moyes's *Season of Snows and Sins* (1971). Central to Martha Grimes's *The Dirty Duck* (1984) is the theory that Christopher Marlowe murdered Shakespeare. Jane Langton has written a series of detective novels with contemporary settings that draw on the lives and writings of nineteenth-century American writers such as Emily Dickinson in *Emily Dickinson is Dead* (1984). There is even an anthology of mystery stories concerning the world of books, *Chapter and Hearse* (1985).

Many detectives are associated with the world of books. Lillian de la Torre has written many stories with Dr. Sam: Johnson as detective. Amanda Cross's Kate Fansler is a professor of literature who appears in mysteries structured around particular writers: Sophocles, Joyce, Freud, W. H. Auden. Edmund Crispin's Gervase Fenn is a literary critic turned detective; Elizabeth Daly's Henry Gamadge, a bibliophile; Ellery Queen, a writer of mysteries; the Lockridges' Jerry North, a publisher; and P. D. James's Adam Dalgliesh, a published poet.

For the mysteries of P. D. James are no exception to this use of books. The title of *Cover Her Face*, her first mystery, comes from Webster's *The Duchess of Malfi*, the play in which Clarissa is to appear in *The Skull beneath the Skin*, a title that comes from T. S. Eliot. *Unnatural Causes* looks back to Sayers's *Unnatural Death*, just as *An Unsuitable Job for a Woman* recalls Sayers's *Gaudy Night*. Maurice Seton in *Unnatural Causes* is a mystery writer whose murder reenacts the fictional one he is working on. The opening lines of his mystery are the opening lines of James's mystery—a neat example of "the book-within-the-book." The device of having a murder similar to one described in a particular book is one Ellery Queen used in *The Tragedy of Y* (1932) and S. S. Van Dine in *The Greene Murder Case* (1928).

James's mysteries are peppered with literary quotations and allusions from John Ford, George Orwell, Plato, E. M. Forster, Walt Whitman, John Donne, George Crabbe, and Christopher Smart, to mention only a few at random. Indeed, the characters in *The Skull beneath the Skin* seem to speak in literary quotations, verbatim at that, from the Bible, Malory, Marlowe, Shakespeare, Webster, Nietzsche, Henry James, Kipling, and Orwell. A police inspector comes up with a quotation from Voltaire in French, the pronunciation of which Cordelia corrects.

Victims in James are often characterized by the books they read. In *Shroud for a Nightingale*, Jo Fallon's library contains books by Graham Greene, Ivy Compton-Burnett, Anthony Powell, Evelyn Waugh, and Joyce Cary, tastes in literature that Dalgliesh shares, a fact that makes him particularly conscious of what a sense of waste and loss murder is. Works by Teilhard de Chardin, Sartre, Simone Weil, and Plato are to be found in Lorrimer's bookshelves in *Death of an Expert Witness*, leading Massingham to characterize the scientist as a man who tormented himself trying to find the meaning to existence (167). A liking for Jane Austen is often in James a reliable test of a character's personality.

Finally, as Charney writes, "The intellectual disposition of the detective crystallizes the values that permeate a particular novel."[7] Dalgliesh reflects both Jane Austen's detachment and Thomas Hardy's broodingness, Austen and Hardy being Dalgliesh's favorite writers. Cordelia Gray's behavior in *Unnatural Causes* brings to mind the pluckiness and intelligence of Sayers's Harriet Vane and in *The Skull beneath the Skin* the courage and dignity of Webster's Duchess of Malfi.

But *The Skull beneath the Skin* does more than recall for the reader John Webster and Agatha Christie. It also sounds strongly resonant chords from other James novels. Indeed, "the book-within-the-book" here is the work of P. D. James herself.

It is not surprising for a mystery writer to return to certain themes and situations he or she finds compelling. One thinks of Ross Mac-

Donald's almost formulaic reliance on the Oedipal pattern and the search for the past; Patricia Highsmith's fascination with the theme of a pathological conflict between two men; Julian Symons's use of violence to point out his feelings about the pressures of urban living; Georges Simenon's variation on the situation of apparently happy spouses who disappear from their pleasant family lives to lead new lives elsewhere; Margaret Millar's concern with terrible marriages, and the insistence in P. D. James on the theme of the indignity and harsh reality of death by murder and her strong sense of retributive justice, her concentration on loneliness and solitude, guilt and remorse. That she should echo herself is not, then, unusual.

What is unusual is the degree to which, as Robin W. Winks notes, *The Skull beneath the Skin* becomes "a playful series of self-parodies" that remind one "of each previous James book."[8] He cites no evidence, but it is easy enough to find. John Webster's *The Duchess of Malfi* figures in James's first book and in her most recent one. Clarissa Lisle is much like Sally Jupp in her trying to manipulate people and set up situations to see what will happen. She even writes one of the threatening letters herself to ensure attention, something Sally might have done. Both women end up as murder victims.

Cover Her Face, A Mind to Murder, and *The Skull beneath the Skin* all contain crimes unrelated to the murder. In the latter two books, Peter Nagle and Ambrose Gorringe are more heinous than Marion Bolam and Simon Lessing, the killers. Both these novels, along with *An Unsuitable Job for a Woman,* involve a cover-up of a murder.

Cordelia's escape from death by drowning in *The Skull beneath the Skin* is another instance of déjà-vu. In *An Unsuitable Job for a Woman* Cordelia frees herself from a well with the aid of Mark Callender's belt and buckle. As we learn in the second Cordelia Gray novel, she considers that belt to be a talisman of "reassuring strength" (313). The same belt saves her again from death by drowning. Somewhere on her trip to Speymouth to secure a copy of the newspaper clipping, she loses her belt. The fisherman who saves her has come back to Courcy to return the belt she had accidentally left behind in his boat.

Not only situations but also characters remind us of earlier James characters. Ivo Whittingham is a reworking of both Oliver Latham and Justin Bryce in *Unnatural Causes.* Like Latham, Ivo is a drama critic. Justin's bones jut through his skin making him look like a skull beneath the skin, a death's head, a figure both Clarissa and Cordelia use to describe Ivo.

Ambrose Gorringe has the same family name as Nancy Gorringe, the maidservant whom Thomas Nightingale, the builder of Nightingale House, tormented until the poor girl hanged herself. It is her ghost that can be heard weeping nights on the hospital grounds. Her story is one of those acts of Victorian sadism that so fascinate Ambrose and lead to his collection of Victorian necrophilia.

Ambrose resembles Julius Court in *The Black Tower*, not so much in physical traits—though both have a certain unpleasant self-indulgent softness to their features—but in their way of life. Both men are sensualists, both are collectors, both plot to protect their domain, both have strikingly similar attitudes toward death, believing "that this life is all that we have" (304). For both men that belief colors the conduct of their affairs. Both attempt to murder the detective who has uncovered the truth about them.

The Skull beneath the Skin even has a reasonable, if coarse, facsimile of Adam Dalgliesh in the person of Inspector Grogan. Like Dalgliesh, he is a loner; his wife has left him. His cottage is as bare as Dalgliesh's flat. Like Dalgliesh, he speaks of murder's "contaminating impact" (158). He maintains just as strongly as Dalgliesh the conviction that regardless of the victim's character, "she had as much right to live her life to the last natural moment as . . . any creature under the Queen's peace" (177). He even quotes, not once but twice, one of Dalgliesh's favorite maxims, one that Cordelia also cites: "We musn't theorize too far ahead of the facts" (231).

Grogan even knows Dalgliesh slightly, having served in the C.I.D. in Scotland Yard until he resigned, disgusted with corruption on the force. He tells his young assistant, Buckley, who is to Grogan what Masterson and Massingham are to Dalgliesh, that when the Home Office wants to show that police have manners and know what wine to order, it trots out Dalgliesh. "If he didn't exist, the force would have to invent him" (232). Still, he concludes, "like him or not, he's a good copper, one of the best" (232).

Why the self-parody? It could be, as Michele Slung believes, that it is evidence that James is merely going through the motions of writing, falling back on what has worked before, pandering to her audience by giving them what they expect. Perhaps her heart is just not in it.[9]

It could be that in accepting the challenge to write a viable mystery using the conventions of the classical English detective story, James included her own novels as part of that tradition.

It could be, taking up on Winks's notion, that James is in a playful mood, poking deft fun at the conventions to be found in the works of others as well as in her own work. This point of view is given support by a short story James published shortly after *The Skull beneath the Skin*. "The Murder of Santa Claus" (1984),[10] like the novel, has fun with the venerable traditions of detective fiction. As in *The Skull beneath the Skin*, we have a classic country house murder with all the props and creaking stage machinery of such fiction. Its basic situation—the murder of a character dressed as Santa Claus preceded by mysterious missives—is itself not unlike that in Ellery Queen's *The Finishing Stroke* (1958), a prime example of the classical detective novel.

The detective in James's story is young Charles Mickledore, the only amateur detective in James's fiction. He grows up to be a detective writer who does "a workmanlike job on the old conventions" (534). His unfashionably old-fashioned detective stories are not unlike those backneyed stories of Maurice Seton in *Unnatural Causes*. The only other detective writer in James, Seton becomes a victim of murder; Mickledore, the crime-writer-to-be, is the detective in his story. Mickledore seems to be familiar with the work of the fictional Maurice Seton, for like Seton's the Honorable Martin Carruthers, a parody of Dorothy L. Sayers's Lord Peter Wimsey, Mickledore's detective, the Honorable Martin Carstairs, is described "as a pallid copy of Peter Wimsey" but without a monocle and without Harriet Vane (534). James's whimsy or private joke—for how many readers of the story will remember the name of Seton's fictional detective—is further underscored when Mickledore acknowledges that he is "no H. R. F. Keating, no Dick Francis, not even a P. D. James" (534). In this light-hearted story that never departs from the cozy world of the classical detective novel James is obviously not taking herself too seriously. So perhaps we are to see *The Skull beneath the Skin* as an entertainment, "a bit of fun, risibly slavish in its adherence to the form" of the classical detective story,[11] but still effective in and of itself as a mystery novel.

Evaluation

The Skull beneath the Skin is well paced. In the first half James leisurely introduces us to the characters and situation. After the murder, which occurs halfway through the book, James picks up the pace with

a series of revelations and confrontations climaxed by the exciting res-
cue from the Devil's Kettle. The narrative line is always assured and
steady and the writing is stylish, rich in details—one of the pleasures
good mystery fiction affords. The clues are fairly, if obviously, placed.
The reader and Cordelia cannot help but wonder why Clarissa, in making reference to the clipping in her jewel box, mentions that the year of the review of her
performance was the very year "Ambrose was abroad on his year's tax
exile" (112). A gratuitous bit of information on her part, but a necessary link between Ambrose and Clarissa.

The solution is surprising and satisfying. One might question
whether Simon, granting that from a psychological point of view he
could have murdered Clarissa, would have stood up under Grogan's
grilling. One might also wonder if Ambrose was capable of battering
Clarissa's dead face. Most bothersome, however, is why he risks the
danger of his elaborate cover-up when it would have been simple
enough, given Simon's mental state, just to take the damaging clipping and destroy it. Still, the book finds James in fine form, justify-
ing the claim that she is the decade's "grand doyenne of mystery."[12]

Entertaining as the book is, it does show how the tried and tested
conventions of the traditional mystery can assume a frightening and
very real dimension. Passion and blood and violence are not limited
to Webster's play but spill over into the lives of those at Courcy Island. Clarissa's death is shocking and grisly, and James's description
of it, like her descriptions of the murders of Enid Bolam, Nurse
Pearce, Maggie Hewson, Digby Seton, and Stella Mawson, does not
spare the reader's sensibilities.

Moreover, James's characters transcend their stereotypes. She most
effectively captures those small quirks and mannerisms by which people unknowingly reveal their inner compulsions and secrets. Hers are
not Agatha Christie's flat figures. Their agonies and sorrows, foibles
and frailities, anguish and pain, are genuine. Chilling as is the sight
of Clarissa's battered face, equally, if not more, chilling is Roma's
animal-like wail upon learning her lover has left her.

James has said that *The Skull beneath the Skin* explores "the psychological springs of emotion and motive."[13] Extravagant in his villainy
as Ambrose is, his motive is real and understandable. In his zealous
protection of his privacy, he differs only in degree from Miss Costello,
who provides Cordelia with the clipping, and even from Cordelia herself.

Miss Costello, at eighty-five, has rejected what she finds unpleasant in life. Not unlike Ambrose, she has fashioned her own "private citadel," less "self-indulgent" than his, but no less "self-centered" and sacrosanct (289). Cordelia guards her privacy. No one, neither friend nor employee, has ever been to her flat. Ambrose, Miss Costello, and Cordelia have contrived as we all do, a way of life satisfying to them. All of them protect it as best they can, each in his or her own way— even, as in Ambrose's case, through harassment and attempted murder.

In the classical detective story the atmosphere is as comfortable as that in a Mickledore mystery. The reader feels soothed and consoled as the writer, with the aid of her detective with his superhuman powers, offers the reader the reassurance that the virtues of reason and logic will triumph in the end.

The Skull beneath the Skin offers no such consolation, holds out no such reassurance. Rather, the book ends on a note of ambiguity. True, the case has been solved and the killer punished—once again, James sees to it that the murderer suffers death. But several lives have been shattered and dark secrets buried deep within a character's soul have surfaced for all to see. Moreover, Ambrose Gorringe is free. Despite Cordelia's certainty that she will triumph over him, as she leaves Courcy Island, summoned to London to find a lost Pekinese, improbably named Nanki-Poo, there is some doubt as to whether Ambrose will be brought someday before the tribunals of justice. The harmony and tidy endings one finds in the classical detective mystery are missing here.

Many of the book's favorable reviews emphasize the "house-party whodunit" aspects of the novel. There is no doubt the book is a superior entertainment. But *The Skull beneath the Skin* also offers substantial reflections on guilt and retribution and the expedients one finds to cope with guilt; it also offers sober musings on questions of intent. Simon Lessing, Clarissa's unintentional murderer, rightly deserves our pity and compassion, yet Clarissa is just as dead, regardless of provocation. As P. D. James herself has said of the book, "In *The Skull beneath the Skin*, I think I've written more than one novel; it can be enjoyed, I hope, on more than one level."[14]

Chapter Eleven
The Short Stories

P. D. James's mystery novels all feature a detective, either Adam Dalgliesh or Cordelia Gray, who solves a murder. But only three of her short stories fall into the category of detective fiction. The remaining stories belong to the genre of the psychological crime story, a common type in contemporary mystery short fiction.

"Great-Aunt Allie's Flypapers," "Murder, 1986," and "The Murder of Santa Claus"

The only Adam Dalgliesh short story is "Great-Aunt Allie's Flypapers," which appeared in a Detective Club Anthology, *Verdict of Thirteen* (1978).[1] Contributors were asked to write a story that in some way involved a jury. James's story deals with a verdict a jury had reached some sixty-seven years prior to Dalgliesh's entry into the case.

Canon Hubert Boxdale has come into a legacy from his recently deceased Great-Aunt Allie, his grandfather's second wife. Soon after the marriage Grandfather Boxdale had been poisoned; Allie had been tried and found innocent of his murder. The canon, an undeniably good and humble man, is troubled that the money might be tainted. He wants his godson, Chief Superintendent Adam Dalgliesh, to assure him that Aunt Allie was truly innocent. Dalgliesh is convinced that to reopen a case so old—Grandfather Boxdale died in 1901—with most, if not all, of the principal parties dead requires "clairvoyance rather than cleverness" (6).

Dalgliesh's investigation takes him to the Georgian home of Aubrey Glatt, a wealthy amateur criminologist, who specializes in Victorian and Edwardian poison cases, to Colebrook Croft, the Boxdale estate where Grandfather Boxdale had been poisoned, and to a hospital in Bournemouth, where the last surviving witness lies dying.

Like so many other venerable structures in James, Colebrook Croft is about to be torn down, in this instance to make way for a new housing development. Although Glatt finds the house architecturally undistinguished, he is sorry to see another link to England's past demolished. When Dalgliesh visits the estate, the insides of the house have already been "stripped and plundered" (15), as if barbarian invaders had overrun and sacked it. James continues with the figure of a military operation when she describes how the great rooms of the house echo to Dalgliesh's footsteps "like gaunt and deserted barracks after the final retreat" (16). As he walks along the upstairs corridor with its curtained recesses, he formulates a theory, which is corroborated when he visits Grandfather Boxdale's granddaughter, Marguerite Goddard, in Bournemouth.

Dalgliesh can now assure the canon that the verdict was a just one and that not a penny of the legacy was coming to him through anyone's wrong doing.

This is a very satisfying mystery, especially given the fact that there is virtually no evidence and no witnesses for the detective to interrogate. The solution is based on a variation of Sherlock Holmes's precept to Dr. Watson in *The Sign of the Four* (1890): "when you have eliminated the impossible, whatever remains, however improbable, must be the truth."

Although the detection occurs in the present, James admirably summons up the Edwardian past with its eminently respectable gentlemen and their "estimable and respectable sloping bosomed wives" banqueting at a groaning Edwardian dinner table (10).

An interesting sidelight is the character of Aubrey Glatt. He anticipates Ambrose Gorringe of *The Skull beneath the Skin* four years later. Both share the same initials, both collect: Aubrey, Victorian and Edwardian materials concerning poison cases, Ambrose, necrophilia Victoriana. Both wealthy men have created their own domains, Ambrose on Courcy Island, Aubrey with his re-creation of Victorian times within his Georgian home. There the parlormaid "in goffered cap with streamers" serves tea (11).

But unlike Ambrose, Aubrey is not at all sinister. If anything, in his Sherlock Holmes tweed coat and deerstalker hat and driving his 1910 Daimler, he is slightly ridiculous. Dalgliesh does not entirely approve of him. He can't help thinking that perhaps his passion for accuracy "might have been more rewardingly spent than in the careful documentation of murder" (15).

The story affords another glimpse into Dalgliesh's character. His decision to take up the canon's request, not unlike his decision to answer Father Baddeley's call for help in *The Black Tower*, does reveal

Dalgliesh's basic humanity—the canon "was troubled and had sought his help" (6)—and recalls for us that Dalgliesh, himself, is the son of a clergyman. We are also reminded, however, of that cold detachment that characterizes Dalgliesh. When the canon wants to contribute some money to Dalgliesh's favorite charity for helping him, we learn that Dalgliesh's "contributions to charity were impersonal; a quarterly obligation discharged by banker's orders" (23). The opposing sides of Dalgliesh's personality are nicely in evidence here.

One of James's best short stories, it has been often anthologized. In 1983 alone, it was reprinted in *An International Treasury of Mystery and Suspense* and *The Web She Weaves.*[2]

"Great-Aunt Allie's Flypapers" is an excursion into the past; "Murder, 1986," first published in 1975, is a trip to the future.[3] It is an example of an infrequent genre, the science-fiction detective story.

The scene is London, some years after men traveling in space had brought back to earth the Sickness which had decimated mankind. The world's population—that of England, at least—is divided into Ipdics, carriers of the disease, by far the majority of people, and Normals, those who run the country. Close contact between the two groups is not allowed, and there are strict regulations governing Ipdic behavior and movement. Ipdics live in relative comfort, but when an appliance, such as a TV, breaks down, there are no repairs possible: engineers and electricians are simply too precious to waste on Ipdics (194).

Since all Ipdics are doomed to die from the Sickness—spasmodic fits occur with some frequency, resulting in insanity and death—they cannot be trained for even the simplest of jobs. However, the government does supply them with poison capsules—the easy, painless way out when the symptoms occur.

When the story opens, therefore, Sergeant Arthur Dolby, a Normal, is surprised to find a young Ipdic woman dead, not from the disease or poison, but from a self-inflicted knife wound. As he examines the physical evidence, he suspects murder, not suicide. The murder of an Ipdic is not a felony; nevertheless, Dolby, a conscientious policeman, who has lost his wife and daughter to the Sickness, has been trained to pursue criminals.

The story may be set in the future, but Dolby's investigation is old-fashioned police work. The mystery aspects of the story do not really rise above the competent. The clues are easily spotted and the story relies too heavily on contrivance and coincidence.

The science-fiction elements are static. There is too much exposition and too little showing. Only when Dolby is stopped by some armed Ipdics do the science-fiction aspects of the story come alive. The marriage of science fiction with detective fiction does not take here.

James does draw a sharp contrast in the story between the England of a not-too-distant future—here, austere, stark, with deserted suburbs, pitted roads, unkempt hedges, and roving bands of Ipdics, who threaten Dolby—and the England of the past—represented by an old country church with "cool dimness," "wood polish," "medieval pillars soaring high to the hammer beams of the roof," and an old lady custodian who "beamed a gentle welcome" at Dolby's appearance (204). The loving care she gives to polishing the brass lectern—much like the time and effort Mark Callender spends in achieving order out of the chaos of the Markland gardens in *An Unsuitable Job for a Woman*—only calls attention to the untended fields outside and to the lack of individual concern and continuity with the past, a lack that James sees as signifying modern day England. This failing is seen elsewhere in her fiction in those beautiful old structures, part of the English heritage, that are in danger of being either converted into or torn down for new and more efficient but ugly and depersonalized buildings.

Though set in the future, there are elements in the story that ring a familiar note. The father's search for a lost daughter echoes similar situations in *An Unsuitable Job for a Woman* (a son searching for his mother), *Innocent Blood*, and the story, "The Girl Who Loved Graveyards" (in both a daughter seeks the truth about her father). Moreover, Arthur Dolby's search for his child's killer is not unlike Norman Scase's for Mary Ducton in *Innocent Blood*.

But the most familiar element is Arthur Dolby. Like Adam Dalgliesh, whose initials he shares, Dolby is a loner; and like Dalgliesh, he has lost his wife and child. Both men are skilled interrogators; both are equally schooled in police procedure. Dolby, like Dalgliesh, holds high the value of a human life, even that of an Ipdic. Although Dolby is described as being neither clever nor imaginative and, in fact, thinks of himself as dull and ineffectual, he does solve the mystery of the young woman's murder. He deserves a better story than this one.

"The Murder of Santa Claus"[4] finds James in an antic disposition as she has fun with the conventions of the classical English murder mystery. The murder of Victor Mickledore, dressed in a Santa Claus outfit, is "as complicated, as bizarre . . . as any fictional mystery" that Charles Mickledore, hack writer of detective stories for readers who like "the old conventions," has committed. The victim was first drugged, then shot, and, when dead, stabbed through the chest. Gathered at Marston Turville, a small nineteenth-century manor home, to celebrate Christmas, 1939, are guests, all with good motives for dispatching the detestable Victor. There is even, as in *The Skull beneath the Skin*, a suspicious butler. Clues, alibis, mysterious messages with portents of death, and red herrings are plentiful.

The solution James provides is ingenious and meticulously worked out. Although she has said that the puzzle is not the prime interest in her mysteries, this story proves that she is as adept at creating and solving intricate puzzles as is Agatha Christie.

The humor notwithstanding, James does convincingly relate the murder to the carnage that was to engulf Europe in the next several years. The killer tells the detective, young Charles Mickledore, that Victor deserved to die because his treatment of the killer's mother led to her early death. "I'll be shooting down young pilots," he says, "decent ordinary Germans with whom I've no quarrel. It has to be done. They'll do it to me if they can. But it will be more tolerable now that I've killed the one man who deserves it" (552–53). It is the war, further, that hands down justice as the murderer receives his just punishment, so we learn, when his plane is shot down by enemy fire. As is so often the case in James's mysteries, justice is served but not in a court of law.

Most of the story is devoted to the young Charles. But the description of the older Charles, "unmarried, solitary, unsociable" (504), could well fit Dalgliesh. Charles is not the only character that may remind one of Dalgliesh. The methodical and professional John Pettinger, the police officer in charge of the case, is like James's more famous policeman. Like Dalgliesh, he tries not to let the consequences of his cases get to him. Rather, he lets them look after themselves: "That's the only way I know how to do police work" (542). Also like Dalgliesh, he doesn't much care for fictional mysteries: "Once you've had to cope with the real thing, you lose the taste for fantasy" (541).

"The Murder of Santa Claus" has its delights in its re-creation of the world of the formal detective story, but it is a trifle, a charming one, but still a trifle.

"A Very Desirable Residence" and "The Victim"

Both "A Very Desirable Residence" and "The Victim" are tales of "perfect" crimes in which nameless narrators get away with murder, only to become victims of their own crimes.

The narrator of "A Very Desirable Residence," an art teacher, befriends another teacher, Harold Vinson, a disagreeable man who bullies his submissive wife, Emily.[5] The Vinsons live in a "small but perfectly proportioned Georgian house" (157). It was about to share the fate of so many old structures in James—demolishment to make way for a housing development—but was saved by a preservation order from the planning authority. The narrator finds the house breathtaking, but neither of the Vinsons like it; Harold considers it a cage, a prison.

The narrator covets the house; Emily covets the narrator. Together they frame Harold for an unsuccessful murder attempt on Emily. Harold is found guilty and sent to prison where he dies from influenza. His will to live, so the narrator believes, had "snapped" (166).

The narrator, now married to Emily, moves into the house. Like Harold, he soon finds Emily's "meek, supplicating beaten dog expression . . . provokes unkindness" in him (166). Like Harold, he earns for himself the reputation of a sadist. Having gotten rid of Harold to get the house—and there is no doubt in his mind that he has caused Harold's death—he "isn't likely to be too fastidious about killing again" (166).

Meekly but positively, Emily tells her new husband that she has left a full confession of their complicity with her solicitor in the event anything happens to her; it would not be in Harold's interest for her to precede him in death. As for the Georgian house that Emily inherited, she plans to sell it and move into a new "pretentious brick box" (167) that will become the narrator's cage, his prison.

The story is economically told in a very dispassionate tone that makes the narrator's involvement in the crime come as a shock when we learn of it. James very neatly swings our sympathies from Emily, an animal cringing from her husband's verbal attacks, to Harold. Petty tyrant though he was, by the end of the story, we understand and sympathize with him, as we watch the narrator being driven in the same direction.

Even more effective is "The Victim."[6] Its narrator is a man bent on murder. A gentle, scholarly man, age thirty-two, he marries seventeen-year old Elsie, for whom "any marriage . . . was better than none" (72). Socially ambitious, she soon tires of him, secures a divorce and marries Rodney, on her way to greater social mobility and wealth. Seeing Rodney as the guilty party, the narrator savors the thought of his death and begins "systematically and with dreadful pleasure to plan it" (74). Meticulously he gathers information on Rodney's habits and routines and carefully plots the perfect murder.

As he wants his victim to know that he is a condemned man, the narrator sends Rodney anonymous threatening letters. Once a week as a special pleasure, he hones his weapon, a knife, "to an even keener edge" (78).

A year to the day after the final divorce decree, the narrator strikes, twisting "the knife viciously in the wound, relishing the sound of tearing sinews" (80). Everything goes according to plan. The police question but do not suspect him.

Then Elsie—now calling herself Ilsa—visits him to thank him for making her a wealthy widow and ridding her of a mean and stingy husband—so stingy that after the marriage he expected her to continue as his secretary, without pay, and to open his mail. She had intercepted the death notes; Rodney had never seen them. Moreover, she knew who sent them: "You never could spell communications, could you?" (83).

Life becomes meaningless for the narrator with Rodney dead and Ilsa, now a social celebrity, gone. He loses his librarian's job and his sense of identity. He takes to hanging out at bars, telling anyone who will listen that he was Ilsa's first husband; occasionally, someone takes pity and buys him a drink.

The abundance of details in working out the murder scheme greatly adds to the story's effectiveness. Nothing is left to chance. There is a great deal of pleasure in watching this well-oiled murder machine operate. The conclusion is satisfyingly ironic, as the murderer now becomes the victim of his own machinations.

James plants the key clue to the narrator's undoing quite clearly yet unobtrusively when she prints the text of the first death note, complete with misspelling. The mistake could have been a proofreader's oversight; but even the reader who sees it as a clue will not understand its significance until Ilsa's revelation later in the story.

In both these stories, a "perfect" crime is committed; in both stories, justice is meted out, but not in the legal sense. Instead the perpetrators become the victims of the women they love and of their own crimes.

"The Girl Who Loved Graveyards" and "Moment of Power"

"The Girl Who Loved Graveyards" and "Moment of Power" are psychological studies of unintentional murderers. Unlike the narrators of "The Victim" and "A Very Desirable Residence," both of whom carefully plan their crimes down to the last detail, the killers in these two stories are not entirely aware of why they have killed—nor even, for that matter, that they have killed. In both stories, a return to the scene of the crime triggers memories of the crime itself.

The title character of "The Girl Who Loved Graveyards"[7] has been raised by her aunt and uncle, her own mother having died in childbirth, her father and grandmother in a flu epidemic. A lonely child who has known little love or affection, she finds refuge in gazing out her windows at a nearby cemetery that becomes for her a source of delight, mystery, and solace (52). Her one link with the past is her black cat, Sambo. But she is strangely afraid of him.

As she grows up, she begins to put together bits and pieces of her family history. Her grandmother never forgave her son-in-law for getting her daughter pregnant. She blamed him for the daughter's death in childbirth. Although her father dearly loved her, for financial reasons he was forced to leave her with her grandmother.

By the time aunt and uncle move permanently to Australia leaving her alone in England, she is earning a living as a typist. But because her new landlady does not allow pets, she has Sambo put to sleep. Though she thought she would be pleased by his death, she finds herself in tears.

With a week's vacation she sets out for a long-planned visit to Cranstoun House in Creedon, Nottingham, where she was born and where she believes her beloved father lies buried. The house stands "in incongruous and spurious grandeur at the end of a country lane" (59). Staring at it, she feels the house knows something, "something that Sambo had known" (59). The rental agent mentions that an old woman had been battered to death there, and she suddenly realizes that she had been in the room when it happened.

Her grandmother hated her because of her own daughter's death. As her grandmother inspected her prior to her going to church one

Sunday, the old woman threatened to have Sambo killed because he had clawed her chair. Incensed at this woman who had deprived her of her father, so she believed, and now of her cat, she seized the fireplace poker and brought it down on her grandmother's head. Once again, she sees Sambo leaping up and sitting on the dead woman's lap. She recalls her father's arrival for his weekly visit. She remembers going to church and telling the congregation that Granny wasn't feeling well, but there was nothing to worry about, "She told me to come on my own. . . . She's quite all right. Daddy's with her" (65). All at once she knows she will never be able to visit her father's grave: he is buried in quicklime behind prison walls.

The story is a minor piece that exists entirely for its ending. But it is obvious early in the story where James is heading, so there is little genuine surprise at the denouement. A further weakness is James's failure to make any but a tenuous connection between the girl's love of graveyards and her grandmother's murder.

"The Girl Who Loved Graveyards" is a reworking of material from *Innocent Blood*. Like Philippa Palfrey, the girl has had a loveless childhood, which, in turn, makes it difficult for her to love others. Like Philippa, she searches for a parent, who, as far as the world is concerned, has committed a heinous crime. Neither Philippa nor the girl has much memory of her early years; both have visions of a father's grave in quicklime within prison walls. But the girl, unlike Philippa, is little more than a cipher. How she will accommodate herself to this new self-knowledge lies, unfortunately, beyond the story's purview. All we are left with is a chilling revelation that most readers will have anticipated.

"Moment of Power," James's first published short story, is a compelling study of sexual repression, secret pleasure, and unaccustomed power.[8] Only a slight plot twist at the end, one more appropriate to O. Henry than to P. D. James, keeps it from being her best story.

Ernest Gabriel, a "pedantic, respectable, censorious" man (174), now sixty-six-years-old, returns to the neighborhood where he once worked as a filing clerk in a great black building overlooking a shop with a flat above. The visit brings back memories of sixteen years earlier. Then he used to return to the office on Friday nights to read by flashlight a choice collection of pornography he had come across in cleaning out his late employer's desk. Those Friday nights provided him with "a desperate but shameful joy" (169).

One Friday night he had become aware of a secret drama of illicit passion in the flat across the way. Eileen Morrisey, the wife of an estate agent's clerk and mother of two, would arrive on Friday evenings, undress, and then let in her young lover, Denis Spelling, a butcher's assistant. As Gabriel stood "rigidly" (171) at the window, spying on the sordid romance, he vicariously participated in what he dimly saw behind the curtains: "two naked figures" moving "to and fro, joined and parted . . . in a ritualistic parody of a dance" (171).

One night Denis knocked but was not admitted. Gabriel knew that Eileen was there; he could see the lights in the flat. He suffered with the desolate boy as his knocking got no response and he left.

That Monday, Gabriel read of the woman's murder and sexual assault in the love nest. Denis was soon arrested, and a solid case of circumstantial evidence built against him. Gabriel had it in his power to exonerate the boy—he knew Denis had never entered the flat that night—but he kept finding excuses for not doing so. His reputation would have been sullied, his job jeopardized if the truth came out. People would have branded him a voyeur; they might not have believed him; or worse, they might have blamed him for allowing an innocent man to come so close to the gallows.

The most important deterrent to his coming forth, however, had been that he enjoyed and savored this newfound power over life and death. That realization satisfied him, intoxicated him (176). The sensation was akin to the feeling he got while reading the pornography and peeping at the lovers. For the sexually repressed, lonely, middle-aged man, that feeling was "terrifyingly sweet" (176).

Gabriel had suffered no guilt, felt no remorse. The lovers had committed adultery; and the wages of sin were death. Their coupling had been filthy, disgusting, deserving of punishment. If he had spoken out, an adulterer might have gone free. Standing outside the prison the morning of Denis's execution, he had felt once more the exultation of power: "It was at his, Gabriel's, bidding that the nameless hangman . . . was exercising his dreadful craft" (182).

That had been sixteen years ago. Now as he stands in the flat, it looks different from the way it did that Friday night when he knocked at the door and was admitted by Eileen, thinking it to be Denis. He remembers her cowering naked body, the thrust of his knife—it "had gone in so easily, so sweetly" (183)—and then he remembers something he had done to her, "but that was something it was better not to remember" (183). All that had taken place a long time ago. Now he is too old to feel anything: sorrow, pity, exultation.

As his name implies, Gabriel is a zealous man of God, excoriating sinners like some Old Testament prophet. However, he can scarcely understand, let alone control, those hidden passions that erupt in murder and sexual assault. Sixteen years after the murder he feels nothing. His moment of power had come and gone. His crime of passion is nothing more than one of those "commonplace" murders one reads about in the papers (183). It is almost as if it happened to someone else.

The story is smoothly written and subtly told with fine details and with unobtrusive hints long before the strong revelation as to what actually happened. The story is notable for the compassion and understanding James feels for Gabriel. But she could not resist a final ironic turn at the end when we learn that the manager of the real estate office that lets Gabriel into the flat on his visit back is Eileen Morrisey's husband. That gratuitous revelation detracts from what has been called an "unusual" story "in all ways."[9]

"Moment of Power" won first prize in a special Crime Writers Association of England contest sponsored in 1967 by *Ellery Queen Mystery Magazine*.

Evaluation

James's short stories are cleverly and intricately plotted, with well-realized backgrounds and interesting characters. Their themes are those she develops more fully in her novels: the sanctity of human life, the complexities of human relationships, the strains and stresses of marriage. She describes marriage in "A Very Desirable Residence" as "both the most public and the most secret of institutions, its miseries as irritatingly insistent as a hacking cough, its private malaise less easily diagnosed" (157–58). As in her novels, the murderers in these stories are more often to be pitied than condemned; the distinction between victim and killer is at times blurred.

One the whole, however, the stories are rather minor efforts. Too much space is spent on exposition and explanation, too little on exploration of the interplay among characters or examination of individuals at moments of crises. Still, the stories are evidence that James, whose novels are marked by their length and leisurely pace, is almost equally expert at this more economical form.

Chapter Twelve
Conclusion

What best distinguishes the mystery novels of P. D. James from run-of-the mill detective fiction is her rendition of believable people in vividly evoked realistic settings coming to grips with matters of innocence and guilt, questions of justice and retribution, the moral ambiguities of human actions, the strains of personal relationships, and the reality of death. Her concentration on the painful problems of being human rather than on the mechanics of crime and detection has broadened and deepened the range of her mysteries so that contemporary crime novelists who invest their stories with introspection, dark overtones, and shrewd psychological probings are said to be writing in the tradition of P. D. James just as James, when she began writing mysteries, was said to be writing in the tradition of Dorothy L. Sayers.

In setting, characterization, and thematic structure, James's fiction represents a considerable achievement.

Setting

We begin with setting for that is where James begins. The setting of every story is as important to her as it was to Margery Allingham before her. What sparks her creative imagination is a desire to write about a particular locale, such as Dorset or Cambridge, or a special site, such as a nursing home or a forensic science laboratory. "There nearly always is a 'place' first," she says, "and to an extent that dictates what one is writing about."[1] She doubts that she could write a successful book set somewhere she had never visited, never known, or one that had to do with a way of life totally alien to her.[2] At the same time, she has never repeated a place as a setting for murder.

Like many English mystery writers, James knows her way around the English countryside; she has a feel for its flora and fauna, its birds, its rock formations. She writes with equally striking visual power of the somber cliffs of Dorset, the flat East Anglian countryside, the rich tints of a Suffolk autumn, the languor of a Cambridge summer.

Her knowledge of architecture she has passed on to her protagonists. She is especially fond of Georgian architecture, but she describes with pleasure and accurate detail all sorts of houses: a late seventeenth-century home with hipped roof, dormer windows, and richly carved cornices that now serves as a forensic laboratory; a Christopher Wren chapel that over the years has been a chemical storehouse, a concert hall, and a trysting place; an early eighteenth-century square stone house that has become a nursing home; a tall Georgian building that now houses a psychiatric clinic; an immense and ornately decorated Victorian house that now is used as a nursing school.

Many of these converted buildings, as we have seen, stand in danger of being changed once again or torn down to make way for flats to alleviate England's chronic housing shortage. At their best, these new structures are practical; at their worst, they are ugly and impersonal and represent a break with the past. Writing of the concern in James's fiction of the changing architectural scene, Bernard Benstock says it may have "ramifications for the condition of contemporary Britain," but, he adds, James avoids "resounding statements and is refreshingly free from moralizing."[3]

James pays equal, if not more, attention to the interiors of these structures. They reveal and reflect the essential self of those living and working in them. The objects people surround themselves with, the books on their shelves, the knicknacks in their china cabinets, the paintings on their walls, and the chairs they sit on "help reaffirm identity."[4]

Matron Mary Taylor's flat in Nightingale House, with its striking floor to ceiling bookcases, its sophisticated telescope, and its black leather sofa confirms our initial impression of her as an intelligent, strong-willed woman.

Courcy Castle, that restored Victorian edifice with its chamber of horrors complete with popular gallows literature, Staffordshire figurines of Victorian murderers, and grisly mementos of notorious crimes, not only tells us something of its owner, Ambrose Gorringe, but also establishes an atmosphere for the novel. The Black Tower, its limestone blocks faced with flaking black shale that gives a blotched appearance, casts a shadow over Toynton Grange, its unhappy staff, and its terminally ill patients. The fens in *Death of an Expert Witness* exude a sinister atmosphere, a sense of bleakness and loneliness that finds its correlative in the lives of the characters.

The setting, of course, can do more than create mood: it can furnish clues to the solution of the mystery. From the rooms in which Maurice Seton lived, Dalgliesh surmises that he suffered from claustrophobia, the key to the way he died and to his killer. The pot of stew on the stove of Mark Callender's cottage, the cup of coffee on the table, and the partly dug patch of earth outside with a pitchfork still in it lead Cordelia to question the official verdict that Mark killed himself.

Vivid descriptive details in a realized setting also foster an illusion of reality that makes the intrusion of murder seem even more horrible. Moreover, that the irrational and terrible act of murder occurs in a setting "rooted in comfortable reality" makes that murder believable.[5] The corpse is as "shockingly out of place," as W. H. Auden has pointed out, "as when a dog makes a mess on a living room carpet."[6] There is no way to avoid it.

Not surprisingly, James's best novels take place within the medical and administrative settings that she knows so well from personal experience, thus lending authority to her sharply conveyed scenes. In all of her books she creates the sense of place that is so important in detective fiction for revealing character, for creating mood, for furnishing clues, and for heightening that feeling of unrest that lies at the very core of detective fiction.[7] Her ability to do so is one of her strengths as a novelist.

Characters

In most detective fiction, characters exist on the level of the conventional and the stereotyped and often find themselves sacrificed to the exigencies of plot. James's characters, however, have identities apart from the murder in which they are involved; they are much more than just a complex of motives to murder. They have lives of their own. They are interesting as people; they have depth and personality.

James writes mostly about white-collar, middle-class English men and women—Protestant, educated, articulate. Her own work in hospital administration and with the Criminal Division of the British Home Office gives her the insight and understanding to write with sympathy and authority about various levels of bureaucracy from file clerks, secretaries, and sergeants, to administrators, directors, and commissioners.

She writes with equal authority, if not sympathy, about doctors, nurses, lawyers, publishers, and writers. She looks upon doctors, for example, with a barely tolerant bemusement. Many have double names as if to emphasize their pomposity. Dr. Stephen Courtney-Briggs is an egotist who cannot stand a single moment without the soothing sound of his own voice; Dr. Lionel Forbes-Denby's patients revel in his eccentricities and relate with relish his most recent outrage or rudeness; the patients of Sir James Grantley-Mathers, whose offices look more like a study than a consulting room, know better than to ask questions that would pain him to answer.

Dr. Reginald Bain-Thompson, a pathologist, approaches his patients—corpses—in a most prim manner, as if he were afraid they might sit up and grab him. Dr. Ellis-Jones, also a pathologist, reminds Sergeant Buckley, as he watches him slice and weigh Clarissa Lisle's body, of his Uncle Charlie, a butcher, save that Uncle Charlie treated his meat with more respect than the doctor does his bodies. Sir Miles Honeyman, still another pathologist, is a genius to some, a fool to others; eminently content with himself, he cannot imagine that anyone might find him less than lovable.

James takes as much care with her minor characters as she does with her major ones. Sergeant Buckley, Grogan's assistant in *The Skull beneath the Skin*, plays a small part in the story. Yet we learn what his family background and scholastic record were like, why he decided not to continue his education at a university, why he entered the police force rather than the army, what his limitations are and his awareness of them. All this information lends substance and texture to those scenes in which he and Grogan interrogate suspects or discuss the case; it makes of him more than a disembodied voice.

What is true of Buckley is equally true of John Massingham in *Death of an Expert Witness*, Charles Masterson in *Shroud for a Nightingale*, Aunt Jane in *Unnatural Causes*, and Ursula Hollis in *The Black Tower*, and other minor characters. They are provided with family histories, social backgrounds, personal lives, points of view.

Even those characters who appear in only a scene or two have obvious personalities and character traits that make them believable. One thinks of Mrs. Winifred Swaffield, the protypical country rector's wife; the slovenly Miss Willard, who insists she is not a housekeeper but a working house guest; the wan Mrs. Meakin, who would rather be dead than lonely; Miss Markland, seething with repressed passion; and Mrs. Dettinger, who looks like a caricature of a stage prostitute and who has only a tango contest on her mind. James's fiction contains a grand gallery of minor characters.

Love and Marriage

Many of James's characters, major and minor, men and women, lead unhappy emotional lives. They yearn for love and meaningful relationships, but in their search are more often than not disappointed, frustrated, thwarted.

Unhappy, broken marriages fill her pages. Divorce is an answer for some of her characters. Others stay together simply because they would be more miserable apart. One couple in therapy in *A Mind to Murder* is preoccupied with the perilous state of their marriage, a preoccupation they will let go only with a struggle. Dalgliesh had not been married long enough before his wife died for him to know how they would have faced the stresses of his work and the further strain of her Catholicism and his own lack of religious affiliation. That the Pridmores and the Bidwells in *Death of an Expert Witness* have remained together is attributable more than anything else to the fact that Arthur Pridmore and Albert Bidwell are taciturn men with garrulous wives. The happy marriage of the Maxies in *Cover Her Face* has fallen upon the dark days of his invalidism and coma that result in the hiring of Sally Jupp and Mrs. Maxie's subsequent murder of her.

Many of James's women would agree with Sister Ambrose's conclusion in *A Mind to Murder* that marriage benefitted men at women's expense. Both Nurse Harper and Nurse Goodale sacrifice careers to become wives and mothers; it is what is expected of them. Brenda Pridmore sees either a career or marriage in her future, but not both. Jennifer Priddy's plans for a career strike the male-chauvinistic Dalgliesh as strange. Surely, he thinks, she has no ambition and would soon marry. The implication is that Pridmore and Priddy, alike in more than name, would give up any idea of a career once married.

Both Mrs. Gladwin and Elizabeth Leaming in *An Unsuitable Job for a Woman* have subordinated themselves to their men. The devotion they have spent on them is not returned or, for that matter, even acknowledged. Mrs. Gladwin sees her marriage as nothing but a job; Gladwin was eager enough to marry her when he needed a nurse. Leaming has given twenty years of her life as glorified secretary to the man she has loved, bearing his child and watching it raised as another's. Sir Ronald cannot get along without her, but he will not marry her even when his wife's death frees him.

Few marital stories in James are as sad as Ursula Hollis's in *The Black Tower*. Her eighteen-month marriage had been shaky enough, since she could never feel confident it was grounded in reality. Now she is a patient at Toynton Grange, deserted by her husband, unable to get around except with the greatest of effort. She has become increasingly miserable, a common enough state for many of James's characters.

Given the precarious nature of marriage in her fiction, it is not surprising to find so many illicit sexual liaisons, so many unfaithful wives and adulterous husbands: James Baguley, Elsie Bowman, Inspector Doyle, Ronald Callender, Roma Lisle's lover Colin, Clarissa Lisle, Stephen Courtney-Briggs, Eric Hewson, Leonard Morris, Maurice Palfrey, Emily Vinson.

"The happiest marriages," James writes, are those "sustained by . . . comforting illusions." That formula, appearing in the opening chapter of *Shroud for a Nightingale* (10), explains the success of the innocent, that is to say, nonsexual, relationship between Muriel Beale and her devoted companion for twenty-five years, Angela Burrows. Each supports and buttresses the other's beliefs about herself. Likewise, Sister Ambrose and her elderly friend, Bea Sharpe, in *A Mind to Murder*, have lived together for twenty years in comfortable and happy harmony. Their relationship, too, is nonsexual. Such relationships were known in the nineteenth century as "Boston marriages," intense, exclusive relationships between upper class single women, such as that between Alice James and Katharine Loring or between Sarah Orne Jewett and the widowed Annie Fields.[8]

James is less approving of sexual relationships between women. Hilda Rolfe finds little joy with Julia Pardoe. The happiness that Angela Foley and Stella Mawson find together is cut short by Stella's murder.

But neither is James entirely disapproving. Philippa Palfrey in *Innocent Blood* raises with her mother the matter of lesbianism in prison. Mary accuses her of making such relationships sound like some contaminating disease. They occur, she admits; people have the need to feel that they count for someone, that they mean something to another person. There is that universal want to be loved (79).

James is not so tolerant of relationships between gay men. Male homosexuals in James share certain "unmasculine" physical traits: soft white hands; pouty, petulant features; flabbiness. Almost all are narcissistic, waspish, unpleasant, well deserving of Inspector Reckless's epithet in *Unnatural Causes*: "a spiteful lot, queers," a characterization with which Dalgliesh neither agrees nor disagrees (53). His reference to Julius Court in *The Black Tower* as "a hysterical queer" (236) would, however, indicate his sentiments.

Gay males are more than spiteful: Digby Seton, Julius Court, and Dennis Lerner are murderers as well; Gabriel Lomax in *Innocent Blood* is described as dangerous, and his boy friend, Terry Brewer, has an air of corruption about him. Peter Courtney in *Shroud for a Nightingale* is gay, alcoholic, and a compulsive gambler who eventually commits suicide. Ambrose Gorringe's sexual preferences are not clearly specified, but in physical appearance and personality, he fits the mold of James's other gay males. Justin Bryce in *Unnatural Causes* may not be as menacing as the others, but this ineffectual, gossipy, effeminate fussbudget is certainly no more pleasant than the others.

James even suggests that it is Julius's homosexuality that leads him to dealing in drugs and murder. Julius tells Dalgliesh that he does not intend to end up like those pitiful queers one can find in any Westminster pub, pathetic men living alone off pensions. To avoid ending up like them, he needs wealth, even if he has to kill to get it (267).

The exception to this unsavory lot is Henry Carwardine in *The Black Tower*. In physical appearance he is unlike the other homosexual men. But then, his love for the young polio victim Peter Bonnington, is not lust, nor is it simply a means to an end, as is so often true of the gay relationships that James depicts. It is, rather, the unselfish love of one person for another. Though the two touch fingers and gaze romantically into each other's eyes, there is nothing sexual about their love; physical love-making may well be out of the question for them. However, any hope for happiness that Henry might have is dashed when Wilfred Anstey, his moral sense violated by this love of one man for another, has Peter transferred to a different hospital; there, six weeks later, he dies. All in all, James's homosexuals get what she apparently believes is their comeuppance.

Loneliness and Alienation

Confronted by grinding disappointments or frustrated by unhappy relationships or tormented by blighted hopes, James's men and women find themselves increasingly lonely, isolated, even alienated.

One thinks, for example, of the wrenching loneliness of Enid Bolam's pathetic life lighted only by the affection Girl Guides give her a few weeks each summer at camp, a warmth her colleagues never gave her. The middle-aged Mrs. Meakin, drab and sallow of face, thinks it better to be dead than alone. Both Heather Pearce and Jo Fallon are friendless and alienated from the other student nurses. Dr. Baguley, caught between a loveless marriage and a love affair that has turned sour, feels increasingly alone. Sylvia Kedge, disfigured physically by polio and psychologically by self-hate, fumes with rage and venom at a world she feels no part of. The patients at Toynton Grange are trapped within bodies that no longer respond to the brain's wishes or to the heart's desires. The faculty and staff at Simon Lessing's school discourage him from personal commitment; as a result, he values the daily periods of silence and privacy there. Ivo Whittingham lives alone, divorced by his wife and separated from his children. Sally Jupp, Angela Foley, Philippa Palfrey, and the girl who loved graveyards grow up never feeling love or affection from their foster or adoptive parents. Lorrimer's love letters bare the loneliness of this man of science who lacks the common touch and whose turbulent life is marked by bald pain and rejected love. Kerrison, his killer, feels that the murder of Lorrimer—motivated by his fear of losing the only ones that make life bearable, his children—has set himself apart from all of mankind.

Loneliness is the plight not only of James's murderers and victims, suspects and witnesses, but of her detectives as well. Adam Dalgliesh and Cordelia Gray are lonely people in a lonely profession. Both these very private people are disturbed that in the course of their job—the slang expression for Cordelia's is "private eye"—they must pry into the lives of others and invade the sanctity of individual consciousnesses.

Dalgliesh's boyhood was solitary and lonely. As an adult he has a reluctance to commit himself to anyone. His poetry reflects his detached spirit. As a child Cordelia was lonely, withdrawn; she remembers only one of her foster mothers with any affection. When she is at Cambridge investigating Mark Callender's death, she feels alienated from her own generation. Neither Adam nor Cordelia inspire friendship easily; neither is sustained, as so many are, by intense, loyal, and fertile friendships.

Their living quarters underscore their aloneness and isolation. Dalgliesh lives high above the Thames in a plainly furnished flat to which

James has never taken her readers. Cordelia lives in a top-floor flat, its sitting room spartanly bare, that no one from the agency and none of her friends have ever visited. At night, as we are told in *The Skull beneath the Skin*, wrapped in the cocoon of her warm bed, she feels closer to the stars above than she does to the city spread out below her (48).

It may be that Mary Taylor speaks for the isolation of James's characters when she sets forth her creed in *Shroud for a Nightingale*: "We are all alone, all of us from the moment of birth until we die. . . . If you want salvation look to yourself. There's nowhere else to look" (82). If one were to search for a text that could serve as a gloss on the solitary condition of James's people, one could do no better than the passage from the Book of Common Prayer that Dalgliesh comes across in *Death of an Expert Witness*: "For I am a stranger with thee: and a sojourner, as all my fathers were. O spare me a little, that I may recover my strength: before I go hence, and be no more seen" (274).

Themes

Beside setting and characters, the third major achievement in James's fiction is thematic structure. She organizes her material around powerful and consistent themes. That death by murder is one comes, of course, as no surprise. For what is a murder mystery without a murder? But there is a great difference between death in the classical detective novel—Agatha Christie's, for example—and in the novels of P. D. James.

In Christie the corpse is merely the starting point for the solution of an intricate intellectual puzzle. Christie distances the reader from death so that one questions if death is a reality in a Christie mystery. A Christie corpse is often dead before the book begins as is true of M. Renauld in *Murder on the Links* (1923). Or else the victim is killed between chapters. Cora Lansquenet in *Funerals Are Fatal* (1953) is hacked to death, yet brutal as the crime is, we never see the corpse; we only get word of the murder. Even when we view the body, there is nothing in a Christie description to upset our equilibrium. Linnet Doyle, shot through the head in *Death on the Nile* (1937), lies in her bed in an attitude that was "natural and peaceful." Mr. Morley, likewise shot through the head in *The Patriotic Murders* (1940), looks in death "very much as he had looked in life." The lady found dead aboard a train in *The Mystery of the Blue Train* (1928) "lay on the berth

. . . in so natural a position that one would have thought her asleep."
As for Madame Giselle, poisoned aboard a flight from France to England in *Death in the Air* (1935), "one might have taken her to be asleep." Even when the corpse does not appear to be just sleeping, Christie's language is so general that her description does not ruffle one. In *Murder at the Vicarage* (1930), "Colonel Protheroe was lying sprawled across my writing table in a horrible unnatural position."

Most illuminating for our purposes is the death of Bartholomew Strange in *Murder in Three Acts* (1935). He is the victim of nicotine poisoning, extracted from a sprig of roses, the same method of murder James uses to dispatch Jo Fallon in *Shroud for a Nightingale*. Strange's death, which takes place between chapters, is reported to the reader through a newspaper account. While chatting with some friends, "he had a sudden seizure and died." But when Nurse Dakers discovers Fallon's body, she knows that Fallon is dead, not asleep, for her eyes, cold and opaque, are wide open, like those of a dead fish (50).

In James we are not allowed to dismiss death as easily as we can in Christie. Murders may occur between chapters, but the corpses are not hastily removed before the next chapter begins. Dead bodies are described in meticulous detail and with striking metaphors. Corpses never seem only asleep in James. Sally Jupp, James's first victim, may have her eyes closed, but, as James notes, she is not asleep. A thin dribble of dried blood stains the corner of her mouth "like a black slash" (59).

As a catalog of her victims shows, death is a very real and a very frightening presence in James. Enid Bolam is very dead, indeed, as she lies "like a plump if incongruous Ophelia afloat on a tide of paper," a heavy wooden fetish on her chest. Maurice Seton dies in torment as he tries vainly to claw his way out of his "side car" coffin; his half-brother, Digby, in his death spasms bites his lip in two. Nurse Pearce, her stomach corroded by poison, screams like a stuck whistle. Maggie Hewson's body is elongated by hanging, her eyes rolled upwards, her swollen tongue thrust out between her lips, her head lolled to one side "like a horrible caricature of a disjointed puppet." Stella Mawson's face is "dreadful in death." Her eyes are half-open, her palms turned outward "as if in a mute appeal for pity or for help." Edwin Lorrimer's dead left hand claws at the floor; the hair above his ear where he was struck looks like a kitten's fur, but it is blackened blood. The one eye of his that is visible is like that "of a dead calf." Clarissa Lisle's face is battered to a bloody pulp; the clotting blood contains fragments of splintered bones. We are not spared any of the horrifying details. We are as shocked as we would be if we came across murder in real life, but as we are usually not when we come across it in the pages of a mystery.

Although James's victims are, on the whole, like Christie's, a despicable lot, their horrible deaths realistically described get from us, if only grudgingly, a pity we never feel for Christie's corpses. Moreover, some of James's victims—Mark Callender, Father Baddeley, Grace Willison, Jo Fallon—are sympathetic characters. Rarely are victims so in Christie. Hers are, as Jessica Mann so succinctly puts it, "expendable."[9] That is not an adjective one can apply to Sally Jupp or Edwin Lorrimer or Clarissa Lisle.

Ironically, the perpetrators of these gruesome murders elicit more understanding and sympathy from us than do their victims—Julius Court and Ronald Callender being the exceptions. Yet no matter how sympathetic the killers may be, no matter how understandable their motives, no matter how deplorable the victims, the bottom line in James is that murder has no defense. Human life is sacrosanct: every human being, no matter how disagreeable he may be, no matter how convenient it would be for him to die, "has the right to live his life to the last natural moment."[10] This strongly held belief runs throughout James.

In *Death of an Expert Witness*, Nell Kerrison argues with Dalgliesh that imprisoning a killer for life does not bring the victim back to life; moreover, the victim does not know he has lost part of the span of his natural life. Dalgliesh counters that the victim has, indeed, lost the years he might have had; even if he were to die from natural causes the very next day, he has the right to that day. One day in a life is as precious as another.

Justice and Retribution

Murder not only deprives the victim of his right to live, it has repercussions on us all. The murderer's story cannot help but touch the heart, for to look into the crime of murder is to look into the heart of human misery. There is a warning in murder. Murder forces those involved in it, the reader of murder mysteries included, to recognize the hopelessness and despair that can drive an individual to take a life.

Murder also invades the privacy of innocent people. In the course of an investigation, their secret shames and sorrows and guilts come under scrutiny. Murder defiles society. Civilized men and women see it as a unique aberration that threatens the very being of society. When it occurs, society must muster all the means available to eliminate the criminal. It is up to the detective or policeman, as protector of the dead person's interests, to see that justice is done. In James that means not only are murderers uncovered, they are also punished. James seems to say that retribution is hers. For with few exceptions, from Mrs. Maxie in *Cover Her Face* to Henry Caldwell in "The Murder of Santa Claus," James sees to it that her killers pay for their crimes with their lives.

In the three years that separate *A Mind to Murder* from *Cover Her Face*, Mrs. Maxie has died, following her release from prison. Digby Seton is killed by his coconspirator in murder, Sylvia Kedge, who, in turn, is swept to her death by a storm in *Unnatural Causes*. Julius Court in *The Black Tower* plunges to his death over a cliff. In *Shroud for a Nightingale*, Mary Taylor kills Ethel Brumfett, who had murdered two nurses, and later takes her own life. In *An Unsuitable Job for a Woman*, Elizabeth Leaming is killed in an automobile accident, punishment for her killing of Ronald Callender, the murderer of their son. Simon Lessing drowns in *The Skull beneath the Skin*; the clunch pit killer in *Death of an Expert Witness* slits his throat; Henry Caldwell is killed by enemy fire during World War II. Mary Ducton in *Innocent Blood* kills herself, saving James the need to find a way to punish Norman Scase if he had succeeded in killing Mary himself. In James, unlike in real life, murderers cannot go free and unpunished.

This does lead to a certain awkwardness in the endings of some of her books with their melodramatic excesses, as James arranges matters a bit too conveniently and tidily to show that crime does not pay.

There are, to be sure, other mystery writers who, within the pages of their books, punish their killers. Philo Vance in S. S. Van Dine's *The Bishop Murder Case* (1929) takes the law into his own hands by deliberately switching two glasses of wine so that Dr. Dillard, the murderer, gets the poisoned drink he intended for another. Vance's justification is that you do not "bring a rattlesnake to the bar of justice" or "give a mad dog his day in court."[11] In other cases, Vance allows the murderers the opportunities to take their own lives.

Most mystery writers, however, are satisfied in only solving the crime and revealing the killer. They do not see to it that the murderer is punished as well. But the scales of justice in James must balance. If the law cannot exact retribution, then the wrath of nature or God or the pen of P. D. James will.

Resolution and Ambiguity

In the sense that the criminal does not escape and that order is restored to society by the solution of the crime, it can be argued that mystery novels have happy endings. The gaping rent in the fabric of society has been repaired. Reason and logic, the bases of civilized society, have triumphed. With the lawless compulsion suppressed, society can once again function smoothly. The solution of the puzzle marks a time to start anew. And, indeed, this seems to be the case with James.

The concluding chapter of *Shroud for a Nightingale* takes place not in the rain that falls in the opening chapter, but in bright sunshine as Nightingale House is torn down. The final scene of *Innocent Blood* begins in the calm atmosphere of a chapel following evensong and ends as Norman Scase walks out into the spring sunshine. Cordelia Gray at the conclusion of *The Skull beneath the Skin* senses that for "one sunlit moment" (328), nothing that occurred on Courcy Island had anything to do with her life, her future. She knows she will survive and truth will prevail. At the end of *The Black Tower*, Dalgliesh is glad he is alive after all. The first word of the final chapter of *Unnatural Causes* is "brightness." The violent storm of the night before has passed and with it Sylvia Kedge, a victim of it and of her own hate.

The solution of the puzzle does not ensure, however, a happy ending to the complex relationships among vulnerable human beings. The law can establish for society the parameters of guilt and innocence. But no recourse to Coke or Blackstone, the great English jurists, can untangle the web of doubts and deceits people weave around themselves. *Unnatural Causes* does, indeed, end in brightness and the death of Sylvia Kedge; it also ends with the irreconcilable breakup of Dalgliesh and Deborah Riscoe: "She thought it unlikely that they would ever see each other again" (236).

The police can pack up their scene-of-the-crime kits and depart, another case solved. But James's characters are left to pick up the pieces of their lives as best they can. This is apparent even in James's first book, *Cover Her Face*. Returning to Martingale, a month after Mrs. Maxie's sentencing, Dalgliesh finds the house "slightly sinister in the fading light" (252). The drawing room has that bare look a room assumes when "the small personal change of living has been tidied away" (253). Deborah Riscoe has to live with the knowledge that her mother is a murderer. She has to cope with both the hostility and the sympathy from the people of Chadfleet.

In *The Skull beneath the Skin*, despite Cordelia's conviction that truth will prevail, one has serious doubts as to whether Ambrose Gorringe will be brought before the bars of justice. Peter Nagle in *A Mind to Murder* is charged only with being an accessory after the fact and not with the graver crimes of blackmail and attempted murder. He will be out of prison soon enough to make Priddy's life with him a hell.

Whatever satisfaction Dalgliesh may derive from the solution of the murder at the Steen Clinic or those at Toynton Grange is dissipated by a sense of failure in the first case and an oppressive atmosphere of gloom in the second.

Certainly the ending to *Death of an Expert Witness*, James's most probing novel of murder, is anything but happy. The crime has been solved and Hoggatt's, like Nightingale House, is to make way for a more modern facility. But the cost of murder has been great. The lives of Angela Foley, Nell and William Kerrison, and old Mr. Lorrimer, all innocent victims, lie in ruins, some, perhaps, permanently shattered. Nor have the murders accomplished anything. Kerrison's children will go to their unstable mother, and Domenica, the cause of so much that has happened, remains untouched. She claims no responsibility as she retreats into the protective shell of her semi-incestuous relationship with her half-brother. If the mystery of who killed Edwin Lorrimer has been cleared up, the mysteries of the human heart cannot be so effectively and neatly disposed of.

Evaluation

The mysteries of P. D. James belong to the genre of the traditional English detective story. The settings are closed communities filled with men and woman with ample motives, means, and opportunities for murder. Like Agatha Christie and Dorothy L. Sayers, James knows how to keep a story moving fairly briskly, how to hint at a dramatic action long before it arrives, and how to make the most of its drama when it emerges. Her plotting is resourceful: she withholds and discloses information in a careful manner, thus providing her stories with their underlying tension and compelling suspense. Her prose, like that of Sayers, is more analytic and solid than exuberant and glossy, but her characters do have bright and witty things to say. Her mysteries also carry a certain literariness that we associate with the classical English novel of detection. Like so many other practitioners in the field, James has a feel for the sanctity of the law. In this respect, her books are profoundly conservative. She sees her mysteries as darkly luminous parables of good and evil. She has likened the mystery novel to a morality play in which the detective as champion of the forces of good overcomes the murderer, representative of the forces of evil. [12] In all these ways James adheres to the form and trappings of the classical mystery novel.

At the same time, she takes the traditional mystery in a direction Agatha Christie and company were unwilling or unable to go. The dark overtones one finds in Sayers are even more prominent in James. Her fictional world is one of vindictive and destructive men and women. Dalgliesh is impressed in "Great-Aunt Allie's Flypapers" that Canon Boxdale "had managed to live to seventy-one in a carnivorous world in which gentleness, humility, and unworldliness are hardly conducive to survival, let alone success" (2). Father Baddeley, Grace Willison, and Mark Callender, James's "good" people, are not so fortunate. They are all murdered. Even the scrupulous canon turns out to be an unintentional murderer.

Her murders take place against a backdrop of adultery, homosexuality, incest, and blackmail. Her characters live not only under the stress of murder but also under the tensions of daily life. Many attempt to find some means by which to cope. Sometimes these means do not work. Then a character may be driven to murder or may become the victim of murder. If murderers, they feel even more pressure; if victims, they die excruciatingly.

This only reminds us that pain and suffering, both bodily and psychological, are the lot of her characters. The words that Thomas Hardy, one of her favorite authors, writes at the end of *The Mayor of Casterbridge* (1886) seem appropriate to describe James's world: "Happiness was but the occasional episode in a general drama of pain."

Nor does Adam Dalgliesh emerge unscathed from his cases. The injury he receives at the hands of Sister Brumfett leaves him weak with nausea and pain. But that physical pain is nothing like the emotional pain he feels in the bleak knowledge that the murderer he has pursued is a woman he tremendously admires, perhaps even loves. Physically and emotionally, James's characters are vulnerable.

There is nothing reassuring about the conclusions to James's novels. In an early mystery in the series, Dalgliesh muses that perhaps there may be some cases better left unsolved, some secrets best kept hidden, some pasts better left buried. Murder, as James reminds us time and again, is a contaminating crime. The splash it makes quickly disappears with the solution. But the ripples spread to create more ripples. In the sense that James's mysteries end with the successful solution to the crime, they may be said to end in resolution. But in the sense that uncertainties and doubts remain, they may be said to end in ambiguity.[13]

Not all her books are equally successful, though only *Unnatural Causes* is a failure; and *Innocent Blood* reveals an alarming tendency to confuse seriousness of intent with a self-conscious literary tone that results in an air of artificiality. But *A Mind to Murder, Shroud for a Nightingale, An Unsuitable Job for a Woman*, and *Death of an Expert Witness* work successfully both as novels of detection and as novels in which a literate writer depicts with psychological acumen interesting people dealing with the painful problems of living and dying in the context of fully realized narrative worlds.

Notes and References

Preface

    1. Robert Barnard, "A Talent to Disturb: An Appreciation of Ruth Rendell," *Armchair Detective* 16 (Spring 1983):146; Clifton Fadiman, *Book-of-the-Month Club News*, Spring 1983, 2.
    2. Ibid.

Chapter One

    1. *Murder in Triplicate* (New York, 1980), foreword.
    2. Nan Robertson, "Phyllis Dorothy White Uncovers the Secret Face of P. D. James," *New York Times*, 11 December 1977, 86.
    3. Diana Cooper-Clark, *Designs of Darkness* (Bowling Green, Ohio, 1983), 30.
    4. Douglas Goddard, "The Unmysterious P. D. James," *New York Times Book Review*, 27 April 1980, 28.
    5. Robertson, "Phyllis Dorothy White," 86.
    6. Interview with Jane S. Bakerman, *Armchair Detective* 10 (January 1977):55.
    7. Margo Jefferson and Anthony Collins, "A New Queen of Crime," *Newsweek*, 23 January 1978, 77.
    8. "A Series of Scenes," in *Whodunit*, ed. H. R. F. Keating (New York, 1982), 86.
    9. Ibid., 85.
    10. Jefferson and Collins, "A New Queen," 77.
    11. Newgate Callendar, *New York Times Book Review*, 13 November 1977, 67.
    12. Jessica Mann, "The Suspense Novel," in *Whodunit*, ed. H. R. F. Keating (New York: Van Nostrand Reinhold, 1982), 56.
    13. Interview with Annette Snowdon, *Toronto Globe & Mail*, 2 December 1978, 37.
    14. Foreword to *Dorothy L. Sayers*, by James Brabazon (New York, 1981), xv.
    15. Bakerman interview, 56.
    16. Carla Heffner, "Tea and Perfidy: P. D. James and the Gentle 'Art of Murder,' " *Washington Post*, 30 April 1980, sec. E: 13.
    17. Ibid.; Snowdon interview, 37; Cooper-Clark, *Designs*, 18.
    18. Jefferson and Collins, "A New Queen," 77.
    19. Heffner, "Tea and Perfidy," 13.

20. "The Heart-Pounding Pleasure of Whodunits," *Family Weekly*, 22 August 1982, 7.

21. Robertson, "Phyllis Dorothy White," 86.

22. "The Heart-Pounding Pleasure," 7.

23. Ibid., 6–7.

24. Ibid., 6; James, foreword to Dorothy L. *Sayers*, xiv; "A Series of Scenes," 85.

25. Jacques Barzun, "Not 'Whodunit?' but 'How?' " *Saturday Review of Literature*, 4 November 1944, 9.

26. Bakerman interview, 56.

27. "A Fictional Prognosis," in *Murder Ink*, ed. Dilys Winn (New York, 1977), 340.

28. Bannon, "PW Interviews," 9.

29. *Crime Times Three* (New York, 1979), vi.

30. Ibid., vii.

31. Ibid., v.

32. Bakerman interview, 56.

33. Ibid., 55.

34. "The Heart-Pounding Pleasure," 6.

35. Bakerman interview, 57.

36. Quoted in Michele Slung, "Women in Detective Fiction," in *The Mystery Story*, ed. John Ball (San Diego: University Extension, University of California, San Diego, 1976), 129.

37. Robert Barnard, "The English Detective Story," in *Whodunit*, ed. H. R. F. Keating (New York: Van Nostrand Reinhold, 1982), 34.

38. Foreword to Dorothy L. *Sayers*, xv.

39. Bernard Benstock, "The Clinical World of P. D. James," in *Twentieth-Century Women Novelists*, ed. Thomas F. Staley (Totowa, N.J., 1982), 128.

40. "The Heart-Pounding Pleasure," 6.

41. Ibid.

42. Ibid.

Chapter Two

1. *Cover Her Face* (New York, 1966). Further references will be given in the text.

2. Jacques Barzun and Wendell Hertig Taylor, eds., *Fifty Classics of Crime Fiction 1950–1975: Cover Her Face* (New York, 1983), introduction.

3. In *Cover Her Face*, James spells his name "Dalgleish." In subsequent books she spells it "Dalgliesh." The latter spelling will be used throughout.

4. Robin W. Winks, *Modus Operandi* (Boston, 1982), 106.

5. "In Mystery Fiction, Rooms Furnished One Clue at a Time," *New York Times*, 25 August 1983, sec. C:1.

6. Interview with Patricia Craig, *Times Literary Supplement*, 5 June 1981, 642.

7. Cooper-Clark, *Designs*, 21.

8. *Crime Times Three*, vi.

9. Anthony Boucher, *New York Times Book Review*, 24 July 1966, 21.

10. Jacques Barzun and Wendell Hertig Taylor, *A Catalogue of Crime* (New York: Harper & Row, 1971), 253.

11. *Crime Times Three*, v.

Chapter Three

1. *A Mind to Murder* (New York, 1967). Further references will be given in the text.

2. S. S. Van Dine, "Twenty Rules for Writing Detective Stories," in *The Art of the Mystery Story*, ed. Howard Haycraft (New York: Grosset & Dunlap, 1946), 191.

3. Quoted in Margaret Cannon, "The Mistress of Domestic Malice," *MacLeans*, 30 June 1980, 50.

4. *Times Literary Supplement*, 13 December 1974, 1419; *New York Times Book Review*, 12 March 1967, 30.

5. *Crime Times Three*, v.

Chapter Four

1. *Unnatural Causes* (New York, 1967). Further references will be given in the text.

2. Richard Smyer, "P. D. James: Crime and the Human Condition," *Clues* 3 (Spring/Summer 1982):51.

3. Craig interview, 642.

4. *Murder in Triplicate*, foreword.

5. Hanna Charney, *The Detective Novel of Manners* (East Brunswick, N.J., 1981), 8.

6. Ibid., 7.

7. Benstock, "Clinical World," 122.

8. Cooper-Clark, *Designs*, 28.

9. Erlene Hubly, "Adam Dalgliesh: Byronic Hero," *Clues* 3 (Fall/Winter 1982):42.

10. Bakerman interview, 56.

Chapter Five

1. *Shroud for a Nightingale* (New York, 1971). Further references will be given in the text.

2. "A Fictional Prognosis," 340.
3. Ibid.
4. Ibid., 339.
5. Hubly, "Adam Dalgliesh," 45.
6. Cooper-Clark, *Designs* 18.
7. Bakerman interview, 56.
8. Norma Siebenheller, *P. D. James* (New York, 1981), 35.
9. Robin W. Winks, *New Republic*, 31 July 1976, 32; *New York Times Book Review*, 22 January 1972, 42.

Chapter Six

1. *An Unsuitable Job for a Woman* (New York, 1973). Further references will be given in the text.
2. Lillian de la Torre, "Cordelia Gray: The Thinking Man's Heroine," in *Murderess Ink*, ed. Dilys Winn (New York, 1979), 113.
3. Bill Ott, "Crime's Reigning Queen—P. D. James," *Openers*, Winter 1983, 12.
4. *New Yorker*, 23 July 1973, 80.
5. Ott, "Crime's Reigning Queen," 12.
6. Bakerman interview, 92.
7. *New York Times Book Review*, 22 April 1973, 24; John Welcome, *Spectator* 229 (23 September 1972):1011.
8. Craig interview, 643.
9. *Crime Times Three*, vi.
10. "Ought Adam to Marry Cordelia?" in *Murder Ink*, ed. Dilys Winn (New York, 1977), 69.
11. Ibid.
12. Ott, "Crime's Reigning Queen," 12.
13. S. L. Clark, "*Gaudy Night*'s Legacy: P. D. James' *An Unsuitable Job for a Woman*," *Sayers Review* 4 (September 1980):3.
14. Ibid., 4. See also SueEllen Campbell, "The Detective Heroine and the Death of Her Hero: Dorothy Sayers to P. D. James," *Modern Fiction Studies* 29 (Autumn 1983):498.
15. Craig interview, 642.
16. "The Heart-Pounding Pleasure," 6. Bernard Benstock sees the Ross MacDonald approach in *Unnatural Causes* as well. Benstock, "Clinical World," 124.
17. Clark, "*Gaudy Night*'s Legacy," 9.
18. Diane Johnson, *Dashiell Hammett* (New York: Random House, 1983), xix.
19. Welcome, *Spectator*, 1011.

Chapter Seven

1. *Murder in Triplicate*, foreword.
2. *The Black Tower* (New York, 1975). Further references will be given in the text.
3. *New York Times Book Review*, 23 November 1975, 52.
4. Marghanita Laski, *Listener* 93 (5 June 1975):748.
5. Jefferson and Collins, "A New Queen," 77.
6. Hubly, "Adam Dalgliesh," 41.
7. Robin W. Winks, "Murder and Dying," *New Republic*, 31 July 1976, 32.
8. Ibid.
9. *Murder in Triplicate*, foreword.
10. Ibid.

Chapter Eight

1. *Death of an Expert Witness* (New York, 1977). Further references will be given in the text.
2. Bruce Harkness, "P. D. James," in *Essays on Detective Fiction*, ed. Bernard Benstock (London, 1983), 128.
3. Erlene Hubly, "The Formula Challenged: The Novels of P. D. James," *Modern Fiction Studies* 29 (Autumn 1983):520.
4. Jefferson and Collins, "A New Queen," 77; Robin W. Winks, "The Sordid Truth: Four Cases," in *Detective Fiction*, ed. Robin W. Winks (Englewood Cliffs, N.J.: Prentice-Hall, 1980), 218n.

Chapter Nine

1. Cooper-Clark, *Designs*, 31.
2. *Innocent Blood* (New York, 1980). Further references will be given in the text.
3. Cooper-Clark, *Designs*, 31.
4. Martha Duffy, *Time*, 26 May 1980, 92; Julian Symons, *New York Review of Books*, 17 July 1980, 39; Barbara Phillips, *Christian Science Monitor*, 25 June 1980, 17.
5. Craig interview, 643.
6. Cooper-Clark, *Designs*, 32.
7. *New York*, 21 April 1980, 83; Maureen Howard, *New York Times Book Review*, 27 April 1980, 28.
8. Campbell, "Detective Heroine," 507.
9. Symons, *New York Review of Books*, 39.
10. *New York Times*, 7 May 1980, sec. C:27.
11. Siebenheller, *P. D. James*, 71, 72.

12. Cooper-Clark, *Designs*, 31.
13. Harkness, "P. D. James," 132.
14. Clifton Fadiman, *Book-of-the-Month Club News*, June 1980, 5.
15. Phillips, *Christian Science Monitor*, 17.
16. Howard, *New York Times Book Review*, 28.
17. Duffy, *Time*, 92.

Chapter Ten

1. *The Skull beneath the Skin* (New York, 1982). Further references will be given in the text.
2. Ott, "Crime's Reigning Queen," 12.
3. *Trilogy of Death* (New York, 1984), introduction.
4. Stephen Spender, *T. S. Eliot* (New York: Viking, 1970), 59.
5. Michele Slung, "The Return of Cordelia Gray," *Washington Post Book World*, 19 September 1982, 11.
6. Charney, *Detective Novel*, 1.
7. Ibid.
8. Robin W. Winks, *New Republic*, 13 June 1983, 36.
9. Slung, "Return of Cordelia Gray," 13.
10. "The Murder of Santa Claus," in *Great Detectives*, ed. David Willis McCullough (New York, 1984), 534–53. Further references will be given in the text.
11. Thomas Sutcliffe, "Stage-Managing Murder," *Times Literary Supplement*, 29 October 1982, 1197.
12. *Vogue*, September 1982, 102.
13. Ott, "Crime's Reigning Queen," 12.
14. Ibid.

Chapter Eleven

1. "Great-Aunt Allie's Flypapers," in *Verdict of Thirteen*, ed. Julian Symons (New York, 1973), 1–24. Further references will be given in the text.
2. *An International Treasury of Mystery and Suspense*, ed. Marie Reno (New York: Doubleday, 1983), 198–216; *The Web She Weaves*, ed. Marcia Muller and Bill Pronzini (New York: Morrow, 1983), 489–514.
3. "Murder, 1986," in *Ellery Queen's Masters of Mystery*, ed. Ellery Queen (New York, 1975), 191–210. Further references will be given in the text. See also *Mysterious Visions: Great Science Fiction of Masters of the Mystery*, ed. Charles G. Walsh, Harry Greenberg, and Joseph Olander (New York: St. Martin's, 1979), 497–516.
4. "Murder of Santa Claus," 534–53.

5. "A Very Desirable Residence," in *Winter's Crimes 8*, ed. Hilary Watson (New York, 1977), 154–67. Further references will be given in the text.

6. "The Victim," in *John Creasey's Crime Collection 1982*, ed. Herbert Harris (New York, 1982), 71–84. Further references will be given in the text. See also *Ellery Queen's Mystery Magazine*, February 1984, 6–21.

7. "The Girl Who Loved Graveyards," in *Winter's Crimes 15*, ed. George Harding (New York, 1984), 51–65. Further references will be given in the text.

8. "Moment of Power," in *Ellery Queen's Murder Menu*, ed. Ellery Queen (New York, 1969), 167–84. Further references will be given in the text.

9. Barzun and Taylor, *Catalogue of Crime*, 513.

Chapter Twelve

1. Cooper-Clark, *Designs*, 27.

2. Craig interview, 643.

3. Benstock, "Clinical World," 110.

4. "In Mystery Fiction," 12.

5. Ibid., 1.

6. W. H. Auden, "The Guilty Vicarage," in *The Dyer's Hand* (New York: Random House, 1962), 151.

7. "In Mystery Fiction," 12.

8. Jean Strouse, *Alice James* (Boston: Houghton Mifflin, 1980), 200.

9. Jessica Mann, *Deadlier Than the Male* (New York: Macmillan, 1981), 147.

10. Cooper-Clark, *Designs*, 19.

11. S. S. Van Dine, *The Bishop Murder Case* (New York: Charles Scribner's Sons, 1983; 1929), 256.

12. Ott, "Crime's Reigning Queen," 12.

13. Ibid.

Selected Bibliography

PRIMARY SOURCES

1. Books
The Black Tower. New York: Charles Scribner's Sons, 1975; New York: Warner Books, 1982.
Cover Her Face. New York: Charles Scribner's Sons, 1966; New York: Garland, 1983; New York: Warner Books, 1982.
Crime Times Three (*Cover Her Face*, *A Mind to Murder*, *Shroud for a Nightingale*). New York: Charles Scribner's Sons, 1979.
Death of an Expert Witness. New York: Charles Scribner's Sons, 1977; New York: Warner Books, 1982.
Innocent Blood. New York: Charles Scribner's Sons, 1980; New York: Warner Books, 1982.
The Maul and the Pear Tree. New York: Mysterious Press, 1986. In collaboration with Thomas A. Critchley.
A Mind to Murder. New York: Charles Scribner's Sons, 1967; New York: Warner Books, 1982.
Murder in Triplicate (*Unnatural Causes*, *An Unsuitable Job for a Woman*, *The Black Tower*). New York: Charles Scribner's Sons, 1980.
Shroud for a Nightingale. New York: Charles Scribner's Sons, 1971; New York: Warner Books, 1982.
The Skull beneath the Skin. New York: Charles Scribner's Sons, 1982; New York: Warner Books, 1983.
Trilogy of Death (*Death of an Expert Witness*, *Innocent Blood*, *The Skull beneath the Skin*). New York: Charles Scribner's Sons, 1984.
Unnatural Causes. New York: Charles Scribner's Sons, 1967; New York: Warner Books, 1982.
An Unsuitable Job for a Woman. New York: Charles Scribner's Sons, 1973; New York: Warner Books, 1982.

2. Stories
"The Girl Who Loved Graveyards." In *Winter's Crimes 15*, edited by George Harding, 51–65. New York: St. Martin's, 1984.
"Great-Aunt Allie's Flypapers." In *Verdict of Thirteen*, edited by Julian Symons, 1–24. New York: Harper & Row, 1978.
"Moment of Power." In *Ellery Queen's Murder Menu*, edited by Ellery Queen, 167–84. New York: World, 1969.

"Murder, 1986." In *Ellery Queen's Masters of Mystery*, edited by Ellery Queen, 191–210. New York: Dial, 1975.
"The Murder of Santa Claus." In *Great Detectives*, edited by David Willis Mc-Cullough, 534–53. New York: Pantheon, 1984.
"A Very Desirable Residence." In *Winter's Crimes 8*, edited by Hilary Watson, 154–67. New York: St. Martin's, 1977.
"The Victim." In *John Creasey's Crime Collection 1982*, edited by Herbert Harris, 71–84. New York: St. Martin's, 1982.

3. Articles and Forewords
"Dorothy L. Sayers: From Puzzle to Novel." In *Crime Writers: Reflections on Crime Fiction*, edited by H. R. F. Keating, 64–75. London: BBC Publications, 1978.
"A Fictional Prognosis." In *Murder Ink*, edited by Dilys Winn, 339–42. New York: Workman, 1977.
Foreword to *Dorothy L. Sayers*, by James Brabazon. New York: Charles Scribner's Sons, 1981.
"The Heart-Pounding Pleasure of Whodunits." *Family Weekly*, 22 August 1982, 6–8.
"In Mystery Fiction, Rooms Furnished One Clue at a Time." *New York Times*, 25 August 1983, sec. C, 1 and 12.
"Murder Most Foul." *Observer* (London), 24 October 1982, 27.
"Ought Adam to Marry Cordelia?" In *Murder Ink*, edited by Dilys Winn, 68–69. New York: Workman, 1977.
"A Series of Scenes." In *Whodunit*, edited by H. R. F. Keating, 85–86. New York: Van Nostrand Reinhold, 1982.

SECONDARY SOURCES

1. Books and Parts of Books
Barzun, Jacques, and Wendell Hertig Taylor. Introduction to *Cover Her Face*, New York: Garland, 1983. See the book as one of her best.
Benstock, Bernard. "The Clinical World of P. D. James." In *Twentieth-Century Women Novelists*, edited by Thomas F. Staley, 104–29. Totowa, New Jersey: Barnes & Noble, 1982. Critical assessment emphasizing character and setting.
Charney, Hanna. *The Detective Novel of Manners*. East Brunswick, N.J.: Farleigh Dickinson, 1981. Finds in mysteries elements belonging to the novel of manners.
Cooper-Clark, Diana. *Designs of Darkness: Interviews with Detective Novelists*, 15–32. Bowling Green, Ohio: Bowling Green State University Popular Press, 1983. An important interview.

Craig, Patricia, and Mary Cadogan. *The Lady Investigates: Women Detectives and Spies in Fiction*. London: Victor Gollancz, 1981. See Cordelia Gray as a character of substance.

Harkness, Bruce. "P. D. James." In *Essays on Detective Fiction*, edited by Bernard Benstock, 119–41. London: Macmillan, 1983. Places James within the mode of the classic detective novel.

Heilbrun, Carolyn G. "P. D. James." In *Twentieth-Century Crime and Mystery Writers*, edited by John M. Reilly, 855–57. New York: St. Martin's, 1980. Brief assessment.

Joyner, Nancy Carol. "P. D. James." In *10 Women of Mystery*, edited by Earl F. Bargainnier, 107–23. Bowling Green, Ohio: Bowling Green State University Popular Press, 1981. Examines those elements of content and style that make James's writing distinctive.

Siebenheller, Norma. *P. D. James*. New York: Ungar, 1981. The only full-length book on James and an important work for any study of her work. Contains a useful bibliography of book reviews of James's novels.

Slung, Michele, ed. *Crime on Her Mind*. New York: Pantheon, 1975. An anthology of stories featuring female sleuths with a reference to Cordelia Gray in the introduction.

Winks, Robin W. *Modus Operandi*. Boston: David R. Godine, 1982. An erudite, witty discussion of detective fiction with several references to James.

2. Articles

Bakerman, Jane S. Interview with P. D. James. *Armchair Detective* 10 (January 1977):55–57, 92.

Bannon, Barbara. "PW Interviews P. D. James." *Publishers Weekly* 209 (5 January 1976):8–9.

Campbell, SueEllen. "The Detective Heroine and the Death of Her Hero: Dorothy Sayers to P. D. James." *Modern Fiction Studies* 29 (Autumn 1983):497–510. Discusses the problems and potentialities of detectives who are young and female.

Cannon, Margaret. "The Mistress of Domestic Malice." *MacLeans*, 30 June 1980, 50. Quotes James on Agatha Christie.

Clark, S. L. "*Gaudy Night's* Legacy: P. D. James' *An Unsuitable Job for a Woman*." *Sayers Review* 4 (September 1980):1–12. James's novel builds on the foundation of Sayers's.

Craig, Patricia. Interview with P. D. James. *Times Literary Supplement*, 5 June 1981, 642–43.

Fadiman, Clifton. "*Innocent Blood* by P. D. James." *Book-of-the-Month Club News*, June 1980, 3–5. An evaluation.

Fuller, Edmund. "A Talk with the English Novelist P. D. James." *Wall Street Journal*, 3 June 1980, 22. An interview.

Goddard, Douglas. "The Unmysterious P. D. James." *New York Times Book Review*, 27 April 1980, 28. Brief account of James's career.

Heffner, Carla. "Tea and Perfidy: P. D. James and the Gentle 'Art of Murder.' " *Washington Post*, 30 April 1980, sec. E:1, 13. James's fiction against the background of the classic detective novel.

Heilbrun, Carolyn G. "A Feminist Looks at Women in Detective Fiction." *Graduate Woman* 74 (July/August 1980):15–21. Sees a relationship between Cordelia Gray and Marian Halcombe in Wilkie Collins's *The Woman in White*.

Hubly, Erlene. "Adam Dalgliesh: Byronic Hero." *Clues* 3 (Fall/Winter 1982):40–46. By seeing Adam Dalgliesh in the tradition of the Byronic hero, accounts for his fascination for readers.

————. "The Formula Challenged: The Novels of P. D. James." *Modern Fiction Studies* 29 (Autumn 1983):511–21. James's novels, although cast in the mold of the classic detective story, contain elements that challenge that form.

Jefferson, Margo, and **Anthony Collins.** "A New Queen of Crime." *Newsweek*, 23 January 1978, 77–78. Brief look at James's career upon the publication of *Death of an Expert Witness*.

Lask, Thomas. "Another Aspect of a Mysterious Writer." *New York Times*, 8 February 1980, sec. C:27. A factual note.

Ott, Bill. "Crime's Reigning Queen—P. D. James." *Openers*, Winter 1983, 12. An interview.

Robertson, Nan. "Phyllis Dorothy White Uncovers the Secret Face of P. D. James." *New York Times*, 11 December 1977, 86. An interview.

Sheed, Wilfrid. "P. D. James: *The Skull beneath the Skin*." *Book-of-the-Month Club News*, October 1982, 3–4. An evaluation.

Slung, Michele. "The Return of Cordelia Gray." *Washington Post Book World*, 19 September 1982, 11. An examination of *The Skull beneath the Skin* and other recent James novels.

Smyer, Richard I. "P. D. James: Crime and the Human Condition." *Clues* 3 (Spring/Summer 1982):49–61. An impressive if overly ingenious examination of James's mysteries with particular reference to literary references in her work.

Snowdon, Annette. Interview with P. D. James. *Toronto Globe & Mail*, 2 December 1978, 37.

Torre de la, Lillian. "Cordelia Gray: The Thinking Man's Heroine." In *Murderess Ink*, edited by Dilys Winn, 111–13. New York: Workman, 1979. An appreciation of Cordelia Gray.

Winks, Robin W. "Murder and Dying." *New Republic*, 31 July 1976, 31–32. Evaluation of James's work up to and including *The Black Tower*.

Wyndham, Francis. "The Civilized Art of Murder." *Times Literary Supplement*, 13 December 1974, 1419. Brief account of James's work up to and including *An Unsuitable Job for a Woman*.

Index